W9-CHD-545

The

COMPASSIONATE
SAMURAI

Being Extraordinary In An Ordinary World

BRIAN KLEMMER

FOGHORN
PUBLISHERS

The Compassionate Samurai: Being Extraordinary in an Ordinary World

ISBN-13: 978-0-9779452-9-0
ISBN-10: 0-9779452-9-4

Brian Klemmer can be reached at:
Klemmer & Associates, Inc
1340 Commerce Street, Suite G
Petaluma, CA 94954
800-577-5447
www.klemmer.com

Foghorn Publishers
P.O. Box 8286
Manchester, CT 06040-0286
860-216-5622
860-568-4821 FAX
foghornpublisher@aol.com

1 2 3 4 5 6 7 8 9 10 / 09 08 07

Contents

Dedication

This book is dedicated to all the real life compassionate samurai who are ethically leading lives with boldness to create a world that works for everyone with no one left out. This book is also dedicated to all the compassionate samurai who have gone before us and have given so much, including their lives so that we could be privileged to carry the cause forward.

Acknowledgements

First, I would like to recognize all of the compassionate samurai who have dedicated their careers conducting, facilitating, and helping to promote Klemmer & Associates Leadership Seminars all over the world. They conscientiously live their lives by very high standards and principles, which benefits others and also themselves. Their example helped to provide the depth in the pages in this book, making this book a continual living work in progress rather than simply words on a piece a paper. They did not ask to be recognized. There only appeal was to you the reader, to live your life on a much higher level as a result of reading this work. There are a few compassionate samurai, I am proud to call friends that are ordinary people doing extraordinary things.

1. Jim Stoval (www.theultimategift.org)

2. Bob Harrison (www.increase.org)

3. Azim Khamisa (www.tkf.org)

A special thanks goes to my parents Ken and Alice Klemmer. To my wife of 22 years, Roma Klemmer, for her never-ending support. And, I thank my children for living up to the high expectations on them. A very special thanks goes to Dr. Aaron D. Lewis for his writing and rewriting this material. To the team at Foghorn Publishers for seeing the value in publishing this book realizing it's potential to touch numerous lives in a positive way. There are many more people too numerous to mention, but without whom this book would not be written. Being surrounded by so many compassionate samurai, I know that I am truly blessed.

Introduction

It is my desire that this book awaken in you a resonance like a tuning fork that vibrates so much you are compelled to take extreme action, you and those around you. In general, people fall into one of two categories in life. They are either nice, kind, caring people, I mean really compassionate souls, but can't make anything happen in life, or they are jerks with heartless attitudes, no values, and self centered, but they are able to make big things happen.

Just think about your high school days. That might be a stretch for you. Just reminisce for a minute. Who dated the best looking girls? Many times, wasn't it the boorish jocks with the most offensive attitude and careless mannerisms? On the other hand, the nicest, kindest, most considerate guys couldn't even get a girl friend at all. Who dated the best looking guys? Wasn't it often someone with fairly loose standards? Look in the paper and read about the endless stream of greedy, non-ethical people from the likes of Tyco's, Arthur Anderson and Enron who have raked in unbelievable cash and then sent to jail for fraud.

Unfortunately, they had no compassion for the people's lives they ruined in the process. Think about those top executives in the tobacco industry who consistently lie and deny the obvious health implications associated with cigarette smoking? How many jokes have you heard about attorneys that lampoon the profession because so many of them have exploited people for profit with little regard to justice? You often even hear the expression, "nice guys finish last" and *guys* is not gender specific.

THE COMPASSIONATE SAMURAI

The nice guy was compassionate and had a big heart but could never seem to get what he wanted in life, while the rude guys, despite their attitude always seemed to have whatever he desired. Tragically, many people have come to accept this paradigm as the way life should be, and as the acceptable way that people should behave in life. For the most part, we tend to believe, (whether we want to admit it or not) that the truly goodhearted people will never make a whole lot of money, have influence, or the honor that they truly deserve in life.

We don't believe intuitively that goodhearted people really make a tangible difference. This is a global problem, not just here in the United States of America. It is why corruption is rampant in third world countries. The selfish people, with the dog eat dog mentality; seem to live the crème de la crème lifestyle. Many people believe that a cutthroat attitude is what you have to have in order to live on that plain. I've written this book to let you know that you can be a mover and a shaker in the business or political world, enjoy great relationships and the finer things in life, yet at the same time, be the most caring person in the world.

If you look carefully, there are many examples of this type of individual throughout history, in all cultures and all walks of life. They are the General Lee's of the American Civil War and the Saladin's of the Muslim-Christian Crusades. They are the Nelson Mandela's of Africa and so on. It is very possible for you too to be what I've dubbed, "**The Compassionate Samurai.**"

If you have never heard of the word Samurai before, quite simply a Samurai is a member of a Japanese warrior caste that rose to power in the 12th century and dominated the government until 1868. They were famous as the most feared and respected warriors of their day. Despite being stoic and totally unfazed by circumstances, the Samurai lived by a very strict code of values, that later came to be known as Bushido, which emphasized bravery, honor and personal loyalty.

Bushido literally means the way of the warrior. The very concept of a Samurai with a kindhearted side almost sounds oxymoronic, yet the word "samurai" literally means, "to serve". In essence, the heart of a samurai is to serve. So I have stretched this side out in coining the term "compassionate samurai" to mean someone with strong values that can absolutely make anything happen, and yet whose whole life is about service.

I believe that with that balance not only can you achieve extraordinary relationships, go to the top of your job, enjoy financial prosperity, but also contribute to others in a significant way and enjoy inward and personal satisfaction. The balance of warrior and compassion is perhaps the most perfect union, where outward success can be enjoyed and inward integrity and peace felt at the same time.

Whatever area you desire to win at in life you need this book as your working guide helping you to embrace the concept of never winning alone, but rather living to help others win in life. Firms such as Arthur Anderson, WorldCom, and Enron would have benefited and still been thriving corporations today if they had read an advanced copy of *The Compassionate Samurai* and integrated it into their culture.

Character is the only thing that lasts. Excitement creates momentum, but only character lasts. Show me a company, a country, or an individual without character and I will show you something that doesn't last. That is what concerns me today with the United States of America. We are suffering from an erosion of character. If we are not careful, the affects will not be like the slow erosion of a rock but rather the swift massive mudslide headed toward destruction.

The enormous prosperity we have enjoyed as a result of our forefathers is in jeopardy of suddenly vanishing. We are concerned with our own immediate financial income while the future of our children's social security fades into oblivion. Some people deal with the problem of their children's education by enrolling them in fancy private schools, while the public school system has been reduced to a baby-sitting machine producing a student incapable of competing internationally.

Our system reactively funds prisons at a faster rate than any dictatorship, yet we won't fund prevention programs in a big way. The system rapes the earth of whatever immediate profits it can get. The anti-American sentiment that exists in many parts of the world is not just a jealousy of the "have nots" versus the "haves" although that certainly exists. It is the juxtaposition of the incredible prosperity they desperately want but that seems to be served on the same platter with no morals and a blatant disregard for others.

Don't think that I bashing my country, the United States of America. I love my country, but I am sounding a trumpet call to resurrect our greatness, sending forth the message that what works for you individually can also work nationally and internationally. The Compassionate Samurai does not seek his own interest but firmly believes in serving the interest of others even if that means that he must sacrifice himself in the process. Please do not mistake this as being a martyr. The willingness to sacrifice does not mean you live from the place of sacrifice.

In nearly every organization there are dominant, take-charge people. Unfortunately, quite often they are the most negative or self-centered. My objective is not to create wimps out of the dominant leaders but rather to influence them not to be lousy leaders caring only about their own interest at the expense of others. The dominant leaders can still win while helping others around them to win also. Calloused and cold attitudes are not the formula for success in the world of commerce, although it may appear to be that way.

And on the other hand, to have a caring heart yet lack the courage to accomplish results is an insidious way of being self centered also. That is just hiding our insecurities with a noble cloak, but the truth is this— we care more about our comfort than we care about the suffering of others. That attitude only leads to becoming judgmental yet not accountable to anyone. My objective is also to help the compassionate souls to tap into their warrior nature so that they too can win battles in life and not have to be limited by their passive temperament.

In this book, I have listed ten codes and will elaborate in great detail on each one that a true Compassionate Samurai lives by (Courage, Personal Responsibility, Trust, Honesty, Commitment, Focus, Abundance, Contribution, Honor, and Knowledge). These character traits not only makes him or her a skilled warrior in battle but also a compassionate fighter and creator. These codes are not practiced every now and then but rather as a daily regimen until they become indissoluble habits.

You will notice all ten traits are character traits. The exciting aspect of this to you is that this gives you a potential *exponential increase factor* to your growth, as

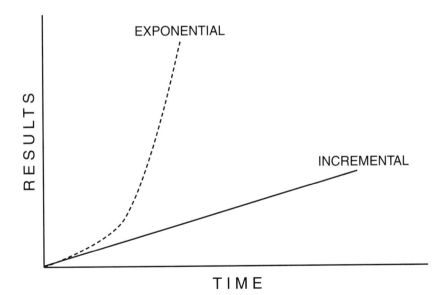

you assimilate these traits and practices in your life. Most books are concerned with how-to's. That's not bad. However, how-to's lead to *incremental increase.* Exponential increase is cause by a change in being-ness or character. If we look simply at a business model you can make an incremental increase from this year to next by simply working harder at what you are doing. Being-ness/character changes cause exponential growth by leveraging new how-to's.

Most people in life tend to believe that they have to choose either riches without a sense of spirituality or poverty and humility seasoned with spirituality. You don't have to make an "either or" choice in life. You can have both! You can be rich and spiritual, wealthy and giving, a warrior in the marketplace, yet a strong willed, compassionate friend to many, including your family and your friends. If ever you have had a challenge on either end of the spectrum, with demonstrating compassion toward others, or with winning big battles in life (the true warrior within), this book is the one that will teach you how to strategically combine the two, making you the winner in life that you were always destined to be.

Brian Klemmer
Klemmer & Associates
Novato, CA
—2006

*A Compassionate Samurai says what
he means and does what he says.
He makes bold promises and keeps them.*

*Average people do what they say as
long as it is convenient.*

Chapter One

Commitment

Commitment means that it is possible for a man to yield the nerve center of his consent to a purpose or cause, a movement or an ideal, which may be more important to him than whether he lives or dies.

—*Howard Thurman, Disciplines of the Spirit 1963*

When people talk about commitment typically there are various kinds of responses. The Compassionate Samurai believes that commitment is simply doing what you say you are going to do. The average person believes in that concept, but only some of the time. The average person believes that you should do what you say you are going to do only when conditions are optimal or conducive for keeping their word. But quite honestly, commitment doesn't have any conditions. A compassionate samurai follows through with their commitment whether it feels good or not. Average people do what they feel like doing.

To a compassionate samurai, commitment means that you keep your word all of the time, not just when it is convenient or comfortable to do so. The historical samurai kept their commitments even if honoring their commitment may have caused them to lose their life. It isn't that they didn't value life, quite the contrary. It is that they valued keeping their word and principles higher than life itself. They were committed to upholding the tradition of honor, which is one of the ten traits of a compassionate samurai.

If a samurai was killed because he upheld a principle such as keeping his word, then the samurai died an honorable death. To a compassionate samurai, death is not the greatest tragedy. To a compassionate samurai the greatest tragedy is either an unfulfilled life or a life that lacks principles. The historical samurai would rather not live at all, than to be alive knowing that he dishonored his name and the name of the samurai. Times have now changed and for the most part the average person today doesn't think this way. We live in a society that has an almost anti-samurai code. This book and the Klemmer & Associate seminars have intentionally set out to change the prevailing mindset of our day.

The average person today could care less about keeping their commitments. The value of the average person's word has become so cheapened that they break their word almost every day. Average sales people promise things they can't deliver just to make a sale. Average parents promise their children they will tuck them in or take them to the park yet feel no remorse when they don't. Average people in home based businesses make unrealistic promises just to get people into their business. Because of this, the reputation of that whole industry has suffered.

When average people show up late they don't even consider their lateness as being a broken commitment. Divorce rates are extremely high for the average person. Corporate scandals are continuously being investigated, long standing friendships dissolve, personal debts are forcing people into bankruptcy, trust is lost forever, and people are afraid to do business with people that solicit them all because of broken commitments. This list could go on at least the whole chapter, but you've got the point. Commitment is the very basis for trust. Trust is the basis of all relationships. This simply means that broken commitments equates to broken trust.

When trust is broken relationships inevitably become shaky. More than that, when commitments are not honored and valued, the healthy process of business interactions, connections, as well as personal relationships gets turned upside down. When a person doesn't keep their commitments people won't do business with them, they won't be in a personal relationship with them, and then the "commitment breaker" becomes isolated. Broken commitments cost huge amounts of money, time, friends, health, and pretty much anything else that really maters in life.

Quit making excuses – Just Say It And Do It

There are many people out there that make ridiculous excuses for why they don't want to commit. They are the *John Average Man* and the *Marianne Mediocre's* of life. In a nutshell, commitment is doing what you say you are going to do. It's really that simple. However, maybe we are putting the carriage before the horse. The average person doesn't have a problem doing what they say they are going to do, because they never say anything! They never commit themselves to do anything.

Just think about how many people you know that never make New Years resolutions. Why do they shy from making New Years resolutions? They are already committed to something else, and that is looking good by not breaking any agreements. They are leading lives of convenience. However, the high price these people pay is that they never accomplish much of anything. They give up all their power because nothing happens without agreement.

Unfortunately there are a lot of people who enjoy this arrangement of never having to commit to anything.

Do you desire to be a compassionate samurai? If you do, you must make large agreements and keep your word. Life seems to work in proportion to the size of the agreement we make and our ability to make good on those agreements. Perhaps you are thinking about follow through and your ability to keep the agreement. We'll get to that momentarily. FIRST, you have got to say what you are going to do. Say it without fear or doubt. Or say it with fear and doubt, but say it anyway.

Now there are millions of people who confess every New Year that they are going to lose weight, get in a new relationship, or even land a better paying job. The majority of these well-wishers that wind up failing themselves are not compassionate samurai. Compassionate samurai get results and continue to stay motivated. Discouragement settles in for the average person who fails to keep their New Years resolutions.

...say what you are going to do. Say it without fear or doubt.
Or say it with fear and doubt, but say it anyway.

After not losing weight, or getting their promotion or financial increase they throw in the towel. Instead of honestly reviewing the reason why they did not make the goal, (which is what a compassionate samurai would do), they trade in their positive confession and goal committing for trite excuses. You have heard the average person's list of excuses exempting them from the possibility of winning in life. Maybe you've even used some of them a time or two.

"I don't really need all that."

"I'm not into material things."

"People who desire to have the finest things in life are simply materialistic."

"The key to happiness is to have no desires."

"It's just God's will."

"You can't be spiritual and have success."

"Rich folks are greedy and don't have a heart of compassion for anyone."

The bottom line is that these are all excuses. They are excuses to not be where you need to be in life, to not go the places you were destined to go, and to abrogate your responsibility to society. Mediocrity is the height of selfishness. Excuses are simply another way of being dishonest. Think about it. Yes maybe there was traffic. But you could have gotten up earlier or you could have told your mother you didn't have time to talk with her right now because you had made a commitment. That truth wouldn't really fly to well with the boss (or yourself really) so we make up an excuse.

Mediocrity is the height of selfishness.

Usually it makes sense. It's reasonable. And now the average person is a slave to the tyranny of reason instead of the liberty enjoyed by results. Vince Lombardi, a famous American football coach, frequently told his players in the locker room before games, "In a few hours we will all be back in here and you will either have reasons or results. What is it going to be?" It is no accident he coached Super Bowl Championship teams. It didn't matter if it snowed, or their star quarterback broke his arm. Those were just reasons. The players became compassionate samurai and got committed to results instead of being average and committed to reasons and being reasonable.

Which are you going to choose? Average people make reasonable excuses for pretty much everything they have failed to accomplish in life. They gain people's acceptance, people's approval and understanding, and an exemption from ever having to try again. Sad to say, they give up the extraordinary life and results of a compassionate samurai. Commit to things that are meaningful to you. You were born to make a difference in life. The only way you'll ever see that difference being made on earth is when you start to make commitments.

In 1972 I graduated from the United States Military Academy, West Point. Within the first five minutes of entering the academy they began to teach us a valuable lesson. They taught us that we had only four answers to ANY question. No other answer would be accepted or admissible. The four responses that we were allowed to say were:

1. Yes sir.

2. No sir.

3. No excuse sir.

4. Sir I do not understand.

If you were late to class and were asked, "Why are you late?" you could only give one of those four answers. It didn't matter if there was a car accident, or if you woke up late, the only response would be, "No excuse sir". I didn't realize what they were doing at the time, but they were training us in eliminating all reasons. Even if the reason was a "good one" like I stopped to save someone's life who was having a heart attack, our response was still "No excuse sir".

That's not to say that we should have made another decision. On rare occasions it might be the compassionate samurai thing to do, to save someone's life and break our commitment. Still, we didn't give in to having reasons. We simply lived with the decision. Most people reading this are not military trained. Many are not accustomed to the discipline I am talking about. Realize now that you are in training for something big. Excuse making and being reasonable will not get you to the extraordinary level you desire. Average people try hard or give it a good effort.

Compassionate samurai do well regardless. Learn the language of a compassionate samurai and make big commitments, keep them, and never offer reasons when you don't make the commitment happen. Jim Stoval is a friend of mine who frequently speaks in our Heart of the Samurai Seminar. He is a living *Compassionate Samurai*. He is the author of the best selling book, <u>The Ultimate Gift</u>. His life story is going to be made into a major motion picture. Jim owns satellite TV stations, has won an Emmy, earned a gold medal as an Olympic weight lifter and won "Entrepreneur of the Year."

He's the only person I personally know who also won the Humanitarian of the year award (an honor also given to Mother Theresa). With all of these undisputed accomplishments, some cannot believe that Jim went blind in his early twenties. Jim Stoval had a very good reason to be a non-achiever, at least a better reason than most people have. He could have used his blindness as a crutch in life, but rather used his blindness to strengthen others, becoming a compassionate samurai, positively impacting hundreds of thousands of lives. You can read more about his story online at <u>www.theultimategift.com</u>. Jim Stoval is committed to making a difference.

This is not to say that you should commit to buying out the Four Seasons hotel chain or owning a dozen McDonald franchises (although not bad ideas). Start from where you are and stretch. Maybe you can commit to being on time all the time for your boss or family. Perhaps you can commit to taking some night classes or a weekend seminar helping you to better manage your time and money. Perhaps you can commit to going out on some dates after being widowed or just out of the dating game for a long time. Wherever you are, that's the place to start. Say it and begin taking steps. When a person puts words to their thoughts, wheels are put in motion that are moving you to your goal. Consciously you don't know what they are, but your subconscious is responding.

A Matter of Life and Death

" 'Til death do us part. For better or for worse. Through sickness and in health"

We have all heard this in the average wedding vows many times. Does it really mean anything to the average person? Based on results we have to conclude it doesn't mean much to the average person. To a historical samurai vows are a matter of life and death. Have you ever thought about being committed to anything as a matter of life and death? A historical samurai played life as if they were dead already. It was a fundamental way of being. This may sound morbid at first, but quite the contrary it is very liberating. When a person plays as if they are dead already then they have little to lose.

Have you ever seen a fight with someone who had nothing to lose? They are incredibly fierce. They play full out. When someone tries to hold onto life then they are hedging their bets. The average person plays life not to lose. The compassionate samurai plays life with full out commitment. Average people don't play full out. They have one foot on the gas and the other foot on the brakes just in case it doesn't work out. It's how the average person goes into a marriage, a business or anything else. They play not to lose what they already have. That's one of the reasons they are average. It has been said that if you are not willing to die for anything you don't deserve to live.

- What in life are you so committed to that you would actually die for?

- What values do you believe in so strongly that you would give everything up rather than to sacrifice those values.

- Is there anything that you can think of right now that is actually worth dying for?

- To what extent would you actually go to prove your commitment to your heart's most passionate purpose?

When I think about these questions it really makes me think about people who were so committed that they actually did whatever it took to fight for the cause they believed in. One of my favorite people was Rev. Dr. Martin Luther King Jr. He led the greatest civil rights movement ever seen in the Untied States. He had a beautiful wife, four lovely children, was the pastor of an established church in Atlanta, GA, Ebenezer Baptist Church. He had a lot to lose, yet he played it full out with the commitment of a compassionate samurai.

> *"I won't have any money to leave behind. I won't have the fine and luxurious things of life to leave behind. But I just want to leave a committed life behind."*
>
> —*Martin Luther King Jr. "I have been to the mountain top"*
> *speech given Memphis, Tennessee, April 3, 1968.*

This is not to imply that a compassionate samurai has to lose their life. It simply means they are willing to forfeit most of what an average person finds valuable and worthwhile. Nelson Mandela is an incredible example of a compassionate samurai. He did not forfeit his physical life, but he gave up

27 years of his life incarcerated in a South African prison to liberate an entire nation. Warren Buffet, one of the greatest investors of our time, has been a compassionate samurai. Buffet has enjoyed phenomenal wealth, but has displayed a commitment to values even to the extent of giving almost his entire fortune of 40 billion dollars away to make a difference for humanity.

Consider how committed the terrorists were on that dreadful day September 11, 2001 when they overtook commercial flights and flew them into the twin towers killing thousands of lives. They had incredible commitment. Not only did they give their lives, but they also planned to destroy the towers twenty years before it finally came down, with one failed attempt in 1991. They gave their life to what they believed in. Quite obviously, they do not qualify as compassionate samurai because they lacked as a minimum, the much needed character trait of service and contribution.

In this world it is the most committed who win.

The cause that some people are willing to die for is not always the most honorable one. It is important for us to realize that the good guys or the most honorable don't always win. In this world morality does not necessarily win over immorality. Good does not necessarily triumph over evil. *In this world it is the most committed who win.* That is why it is critical for the people with values such as; a world that works for everyone with no one left out, to continually increase their level of commitment.

There are literally billions of people in the world who are currently left out. By being left out I mean the 50% of the people in the world who do not have clean sanitation water. By being left out I mean the 20% in the world who lack adequate shelter. By being left out I mean the 70% of the world who are unable to read. By being left out I mean the 33% of the world who go to bed hungry and the 3% who die from hunger every year. There are many other ways of being left out whether it is working on a job one hates or being alone when you want a relationship.

Compassionate samurai consider it an honor and a privilege to make a difference for others while enjoying a great life for themselves. There is a compelling need for the existence of powerful compassionate samurai in the world today. For this cause the team at Klemmer & Associates has dedicated their lives to.

Our mission is:

To create bold ethical leaders who are committed to creating a world that works for everyone with no one left out.

Why some people shy away from making agreements

Why is it that average people do everything in their power not to make an agreement? We have already dealt with those people who refuse to make agreements because they are more committed to looking good by not breaking any agreements. It's definitely a pattern. Some might even say it's an addiction they probably adopted very early on in life. There are some other addictions or things that average people exchange that prevents them from making better agreements and achieving extraordinary results. Some of those low-level exchanges are:

- Looking Good

- Being Comfortable

- Being Right

- Being Accepted

Some people are committed to looking good so they don't make agreements. Others are committed to just being comfortable. They refuse to push higher, or go any further than where they are right now. Do you know someone personally whose main goal in life is to just be comfortable? Many times they will say things like "Why should I do a self improvement seminar. I am fine." Maybe they are fine. However, they are missing out on how much more they could be and could do for themselves and for others. They let their **good** stand in the way of their **spectacular**.

In fact, these people often resent those who challenge and push them to the next level. If in being more you can inevitably do more for others, then an unwillingness to grow is really taking away from others. It is a self-centered selfish attitude. Other people are so committed to being right they cannot make certain agreements. They want nothing more in life than to just be right. Klemmer &Associates has consulted with some companies where average managers were more committed to being right about why things could not change than they were to changing things to make a better and more lucrative working environment.

Have you ever been in an argument with a loved one and charged the other person with a wrong about something as simple and trivial as how long ago something occurred? An argument that little ended up jeopardizing your relationship. Because you wanted to be right, you haven't talked to each other for the past two days, you haven't even been intimate for more than a week. I've been there. Divorce often happens because people are more committed to being right than they are committed to the relationship working. A compassionate samurai has a sense of priorities and does not make an issue of small things when it is not necessary.

Although there is nothing intrinsically wrong with being right, it forces the situation when someone has to be wrong in order for us to be right. In some cases there can be more than one person who's right. Imagine a book like this that had a front cover colored blue and the back cover was red. A person looking at it from the front would say its blue and the person from the back could say its red. Could they get into an argument about who is right? Certainly. Compassionate samurai make an agreement with themselves to live outside this box wherever possible.

Other people shun making agreements in order to be accepted. Average people in the workplace won't agree to large goals because they will lose acceptance of others who don't want to work hard. Many school children do not make agreements to excel in order to be accepted and fit in. The bottom line is that a compassionate samurai never runs away from agreements but rather runs towards them, knowing that agreements are the basis of life and productivity.

The Fear Of Making Agreements

Much of people's hesitation in making commitments revolves around fear. People are afraid that they are not capable of meeting their commitment or they believe the commitment restrains them from being able to do what they want to do. There is an interesting perception that you lose choices by committing. It's true that you do lose the option of doing what you want to do in the moment. But there is so much more to gain when your commitment is kept. At the risk of being stereotypical, many men are afraid of committing in marriage for this same reason. They always wonder, "What if a better option comes along?"

My mentor taught me, "Rules create liberty." Look at rules for the moment as agreements. If there were no rules for driving on the road, you and everyone else could do whatever you felt like. You could stop on a green light or go and the oncoming drivers could do the same. There was no agreement on which side of the road to go on. Both of you could go 2 miles per hour or maybe even 100 miles per hour. Given that scenario, would you have more or less liberty? The answer is less, particularly since you might wind up dead. Rules create liberty.

A compassionate samurai is clear about the agreements or rules when they hire someone in business. They are very clear about the rules or agreements of marriage when they propose to someone. Most people assume everyone is going by your rules even when you haven't made it clear what the rules are. That is dangerous! Imagine if you and I played a game of football, but I played with the American rules of football, and you played by European football rules (American soccer is what Europeans call football). There would not be liberty in the game. There would be chaos and confusion, a total mess. Learn to make agreements to give yourself and others more liberty.

Over Commitment

The people who are over committed are committed to being liked and viewed as nice guys. For the most part they are just afraid of rejection. I have seen people do this in business frequently. They'll commit to doing a job that they don't have the time to do or the proper staff to handle. They are afraid they will lose business by not accepting the job and yet it works in the total reverse. They please people in the short term, but not the long term. There is an old adage in business that you make money by the jobs you turn down. This has several different meanings.

One way of looking at it is that if you accept a job just to be a nice guy or because you are afraid of losing business you will break agreements in production and it will cost you more in referrals. Abundance is another trait that a compassionate samurai operates from and is covered in chapter eight. With an abundance mindset you can say no. You are already paying a price for over committing. The price one pays is usually larger than what can been obviously seen at first. A compassionate samurai pays the short-term price of being uncomfortable, saying no, to enjoy the long-term price enjoyed by being a man or woman of their word.

Everyone is committed whether they know it or not

If you have followed the above you are beginning to realize that everyone is committed. It's just that for the average person they are not committed to what they think they are committed to. That's why the statement frequently made "I have a problem with commitment" is ridiculous. You are committed to not making agreements, or you are committed to not trusting, or you are committed to playing life small, but you are still very much committed. A compassionate samurai is committed to results and the 10 character traits covered in this book. The average person struggles with conflicting commitments between their conscious mind and their subconscious mind are not in agreement on what to be committed to.

A compassionate samurai has clarity of commitment and integrity in that their conscious and subconscious mind are both committed to the same thing. Often times we get a strategy that works for us in life but then that same strategy prevents us from becoming even more successful. It becomes a weakness. It has been referred to as our competing commitment. There are some questions you can use to explore what your competing commitment is.

1. What do I consistently do to present myself as valuable and useful in the eyes of others?

2. What am I really good at, and that I consider a "main strength" that I keep reverting to?

3. How do I appear to others in order to gage my personal worth?

4. If I am really successful, what do I fear may change in my relationships with my friends and family?

5. Ever since I was a kid I was told I was good at what?

6. What act of pretension do I go to work with that keeps me from fully connecting with others?

For me, my work ethic and confidence were how I created my value. It worked for me academically. I wasn't by far the smartest kid in high school or the Military Academy. However, I outworked many of my peers in order to get into West Point, and was frequently on the dean's list once I got there. It worked in sports. I was small in high school being about 5"7" tall weighing about 165 pounds. Again my hustle, confidence and work ethic allowed me to play varsity football, and I even got most valuable defensive player at my senior thanksgiving day game.

I wasn't at all talented. But my commitment to my work ethic worked in being an entrepreneur, helped to create Klemmer & Associates into a successful ten million dollar a year company. In order for us to grow to become 100 million dollars a year company I need to change. We are not there yet as of the printing of this book but it is our commitment. And I've actually written it down here to hold our staff and myself accountable to this commitment. I discovered my strength had become a weakness. When I outworked most employees and burst with so much confidence, it actually prevented me from fully connecting with many of the employees and thus fully capturing their full participation and potential.

Unless they at times saw me with doubt or that I too could be vulnerable and did not have all the answers, they did not feel as if they were needed. So my competing commitment became my need to establish worth by hard work and total confidence to my commitment to grow the company. EVERYONE has competing commitments. A compassionate samurai is clear about their commitment to their principles and their commitment to those principles are always superior to any competing commitments.

For more on this idea, you may want to explore the study of the Theory of Constraints or Samurai Swords, which are made, by a select group of artisans. The real samurai swords, not the replicas, require 80,000 times where the two types of steel are heated, folded, and beaten. It is what gives them their incredible strength and sharpness. The practice of making big agreements and keeping them is just that: a practice. After thousands of practices one can learn and become this first trait of a compassionate samurai.

1. What is the biggest agreement you have made and kept?

_____

_____

_____

2. What new bigger agreement can you make and keep?

_____

_____

_____

"Knock down seven times. Get up 8" —*Samurai Saying*

A man can fail many times but he isn't a failure until he begins to blame someone else. ——Unknown.

A compassionate samurai choose to.

Average people have to.

Chapter Two

Personally Responsible

There is one viewpoint that most people in the world hate to accept and it is this: *everything that you have, don't have, and ever will have in life is all because of the choices you make.* Yet that is exactly the viewpoint a compassionate samurai takes even if he or she doesn't think it is true. A compassionate samurai takes the viewpoint or believes that where you are in life and where you are not in life is directly connected to the choices you make. Average people take the *victim* viewpoint that life happens to them.

I'm reminded of an old story about a construction worker who carries his lunch to work in one of those black metal cans. He opens it and starts to complain about the peanut butter and jelly sandwich he has for lunch. This scene repeats itself every day. Day after day he complains about his peanut butter and jelly sandwich for lunch. By the end of the week his co-workers are pretty tired of his complaining and one them asks, "Why don't you just tell your wife to make you a roast beef or a tuna sandwich for lunch?"

He replies, "Wife? I don't have a wife. I made this sandwich myself." That may sound a bit ridiculous, but it makes the point that the average person makes his or her own "sandwich of life" and then complains about it. So let's build our case for taking the viewpoint that everything that you have, don't have, and ever will have is all because of the choices you make. Taking this position will cause you to strive to play life as a compassionate samurai. No one does anything just because. There has to be something in it for you.

Here are the benefits of playing life by the rule everything that I am is because of me:

1. It improves your experience and what you are feeling, even if your circumstances do not change.

2. It gives you the potential for different outcomes.

3. It puts you back in the power seat. You are in control.

It's Your Choice

Every moment is a choice. Every choice has consequences, both benefits and prices. That's how we start out our Klemmer & Associates Teenage Leadership seminars. The teens will argue at first. They'll say something like, "No. I have to go to school". Our facilitator will reply, "No you don't." The back and forth of "yes I do" and "No you don't" is pretty amusing. Finally one of the teenagers will say something like, "If I don't go to school they will put me in a juvenile detention facility". The facilitator will say, "Yes. That's true and that's called a consequence.

So you are choosing to go to school instead of going to a juvenile detention center." That begins the process of the teenagers understanding that every moment is a choice and every choices has consequences, both benefits and prices. Just realizing that every moment is a choice changes our experience. Try saying "I have to" around something in life, like " I have to go to work." What do you feel? Most likely you may feel a feeling of low energy, feelings of frustration, maybe even depressive states. Now try saying, "I choose to go to work". What do you feel now? You probably feel more energetic and upbeat.

Notice it is the same activity you are doing, but the viewpoint that you choose changes your experience. This is the primary benefit in choosing the power of choice over choosing to be a victim, because you create experience for yourself. Being personally responsible means taking the viewpoint that I am the cause for my experience because of the choices I choose to make. You too will become a compassionate samurai in life when you choose the viewpoint that you are personally responsible for everything in your life also.

You are responsible for how the relationships in
your life are working right now.

Let's go into a bit of detail here. The amount of money that you earn each week, month, or year is directly connected to your choices and you are personally responsible for your income. Yet, I've heard people over and again complain about their jobs yet stay there for years even until retirement age. That's *Joe Average Man* or *Mary Ann Mediocre.* That's a bit insane in my view. However, people do it every day. The quality or lack thereof in your marriage, relationship with your children, relationship with your parents or in-laws, the very state of being single or married are all a direct result of the choices you have made.

You are responsible for how the relationships in your life are working right now. Yet people complain about a relationship for years and pretend they didn't make that sandwich. They pretend they didn't make the choice to date that person, or to ask due diligent questions before entering a perma-nent relationship, or how their attitude or lack of forgiveness contributes to the other person's actions. Why do people stay in dead end positions and complain? First of all, the average person doesn't believe that they have choic-es in the matter.

People tend to believe that whatever life gives them that they inevitably have to take it. If you believe that you are worth more than you are being presently paid, and you can justify your reasons then you should ask for an increase. Yet many people complain and never ask. If you ask for an increase and get denied it doesn't mean that you aren't worth the amount of money that you are requesting. It only means that the employer that you are asking doesn't see your worth the way you see your own worth. The simple solution is to find an employer that does or start your own business.

Many people are so afraid of the possibility of not finding another job that they choose security over opportunity and pretend they didn't have a choice in the matter. If you continue to stay where you are not paid well or where you are under appreciated then that's really all on you. So in the final analysis you are responsible for your economic future. Okay you're thinking to yourself, "This guy really doesn't know my wife," or Brian has no idea how much of a jerk my boss actually is." Listen, I'm trying to tell you that those things really don't matter.

It's not about what they do or don't do, but rather it's all about how you respond to what they do and whether or not you are willing to continue your life under those conditions. That is totally up to you. It is like a ship sailing somewhere. It really doesn't matter which way the wind blows or what direc-tion the current is moving. It matters how the sails or rudder are responding. I now what you are thinking. You are probably thinking about all of the tragic things that happened to you in your life and how they really weren't fair at all.

They happened to you and you didn't deserve it. Okay, after you finish venting keep reading on. It's clear that you have had quite a few problems in your life. What compassionate samurai hasn't? There is no warrior of any sort that doesn't have a list of problems that they can readily share with you that they've endured throughout the course of their lives. The longer you live the longer your personal list of problems will become. When you are born you have problems.

You have the problem of how you are going to be fed, how your diapers are going to be changed, who's going to play with you for the day, and who's going to burp you after you've been given a warm bottle of breast milk. Then as you get older you deal with different problems. You start school and have to deal with bullies bullying you around. Name-calling becomes a real problem for you particularly since no one really likes to be picked on.

When you begin your teenage years and you start to go through puberty you have the problem of your hormones kicking in and yet you have no idea what's going on in your body. Girls and guys who you once thought you hated are suddenly transformed into beautiful angels of your desire. Being cool and looking good is now a major concern for you because you have to fit in. Peer pressure starts to become a problem. Then off to college, and now there's a major problem because you have to study harder than you ever studied in your life.

You think that your professor is absolutely insane giving you fifteen books to read for the semester. The books are each three inches thick. That's a major problem. Exams are coming, that's a major problem, especially since you didn't study. You overcome those issues then you graduate. You've got your degree and you're really proud. But after three straight months of trying to find a job you're pretty discouraged since no one wants to give you a chance. You have a degree but no job. That's a major problem because your student loans will come due, within another two months or so.

You find a job. Now problems are over right? Think again. Now there's the problem of finding the right partner for life. That can be very difficult in a big world with so many choices at hand. You find the person of your dreams, and then your dream ends up becoming a nightmare. Now you have the problem of reorganizing your dreams. Don't forget about the kids that are on the way that you have to raise up, pay school and college tuitions, and weddings for. They're off and out the house and now you want to start living life.

You are never without the ability to choose in life.

Now you're older and you have a problem called arthritis and you begin subscribing to AARP to find out how mature adults deal with their problems. Then you die. Yippie your problems are over! Or is it? They may just really be starting. I went on a mock journey through your life just to show you that problems are always going to exist on every level. The only way that problems will disappear for you is when you die. Depending on your religious convictions, even after you die you may still have some problems on where you'll wind up.

Problems are not a bad thing. Problems help us not only to mature into phenomenal people but also helps to activate our power to choose. *You are never without the ability to choose in life.* I know that bad things happen to good people in life, but how we choose to respond to those things makes all the difference in the world. Even in an extreme situation such as abuse, there is choice. Please don't mistake what I am saying for insensitivity. I am very sensitive toward anyone that has been in an abusive relationship.

I totally condemn all forms of abuse. The truth though, still remains that even in an abusive situation you have choice. They are not easy choices. Each choice carries heavy potential consequences, but there is still choice. There are choices made in selecting the person and there are choices made in how we respond. In the year 68 AD the Jewish family of the Maccabees took on the whole Roman Empire. Put aside your opinion about whether you think it was a good or bad decision or the right or wrong thing to do.

It was a choice they made and there were benefits and prices. They held out for approximately 3 years in the palace King Herrod built at Masada. I have actually visited the place, and it is a spectacular sight. Imagine a thumb rising out of the desert 1200 feet high. At the top of the thumb is a fort. That's Masada. After three years the Romans had built a hill up to the top and it was obvious they were going to capture the fort. The Maccabees met and explored their potential choices.

They decided that rather than allow upon capture their children to become slaves and their wives to be abused, they would rob the Romans of the satisfaction of determining how they were going to die and 1,000 people willfully committed suicide. Again, put aside whether you agree or disagree with their decision. This is merely an extreme example to show that we always have choices. Again, I am not suggesting a person commit suicide when they don't like the circumstances they are in. It simply shows a choice with different benefits and prices.

Even when you cannot see a choice it doesn't mean that you don't have a choice. When you can see choices you have a certain experience different than when you can't see choices even if all the choices are bad choices with limited benefits. Have you ever heard of Victor Frankl? Victor Frankl was an Austrian neurologist and a psychiatrist who was also a Holocaust survivor. This man lived through and witnessed nearly every inconceivable atrocity toward humans, yet survived. Both his mother and father died in the concentration camps. Even his wife was murdered.

He watched people starving to death, scurrying over the one morsel of bread, doing anything they could to survive. Frankl witnessed the brutal torturing of his fellow people, and he saw people brutally murdered. The only relative who survived is his sister that emigrated to Australia. Most people would have given up, or maybe not even have wanted to live at all after enduring such atrocious sights. But Victor Frankl says that he rather chose to discover the meaning in various forms of existence, even the most sordid ones.

It was to that end that he wrote his famous work, In Search of Meaning, which chronicles his life in the concentration camps and how he used the power of his mind and redirected focus to help him survive the effects of the camp. Concerning choice, Frankl under the most reprehensible conditions, still persisted that choice was the driving factor that kept him alive and believes that the power of choice can also keep others alive even in the most trying of times. He writes:

"We who lived in concentration camps can remember the men who walked through the huts comforting others, giving away their last piece of bread. They may have been few in number, but they offer sufficient proof that everything can be taken from a man but one thing: the last of the human freedoms—to choose one's attitude in any given set of circumstances, to choose one's own way." —Man's Search for Meaning

The quality of your life or the lack therof is all about choice. And, choice is all about taking personal responsibilty for your actions. Choice is also about how you respond to other people's actions toward you.

Options and Liberty

Here is a novel thought: **All people have freedom.** What about people who live under a despot dictator? Yes. They too have freedom. Why? Because freedom is the ability to choose and all human beings have that ability as Victor Frankl has so eloquently desrcribed even in horrendous unimaginable circumstances. Note however that the consequences of their choices are far different than average circumstances. Note also that although all people have freedom very few enjoy liberty.

Liberty is the ability to do what you want to do when you want to do it. It is the ability to go where you want to go when you want to go there. Most importantly it is the ability to be what you want to be when you want to be it.

Few people enjoy liberty. The compassionate samurai searches for choices, solutions, and meaning in life, rather than waiting for those things to just automatically appear. A compassionate samurai is all about increasing the liberty they and others enjoy. A compassionate samurai does not shrink from the tough choices simply because they don't like the perceived outcomes of all the choices.

Of all the things granted to us in life by God, I believe that the most powerful gift is the gift of choice. Not only is choice a gift, it is also a very useful tool if used skillfully. There is a power in choice that gives us the potential winners edge all of the time. It is the ability to create liberty. That might sound like a "pie in the sky" philosophy but really it is not. What you choose now determines what you enjoy tomorrow. What you choose not to choose, also determines what you will never have in this lifetime.

So at the end of the day, or even at the end of your life you can be an average person and point the finger at anyone for why this or that didn't happen for you. Or you can be a compassionate samurai and enjoy a life even amidst dire circumstances and create a life of liberty for yourself and others as your legacy.

If liberty is so great why aren't there more compassionate samurai experiencing it?

The answer is because there is a price for everything. There is no free lunch. Every benefit has corresponding prices or things you give up. There are even prices for acknowledging that you have choices (as there are different prices for pretending you don't have choices) and there are prices for making the compassionate samurai choice. Of course there are different prices for taking the easier way out also. At West Point we were taught always choose the harder right than the easier wrong. What was that doing for us? It was teaching us to be compassionate samurai. Some might argue about the compassionate part, but we will save that for another discussion.

If we wimp out and don't make the right choices we lose our liberty.

Frankl once recommeded the Statue of Liberty on the east coast be complemented by a Statue of Responsibility on the West Coast.

Perhaps what he was saying is that our liberty requires us making the right choices. If we wimp out and don't make the right choices we lose our liberty. By wimping out, what I mean is that when a person chooses obvious short term benefits with not so obvious long term prices over a choice of obvious short term prices with not so obvious great long term benefits. The very nature of a compassionate samurai is to choose short term prices with long term benefits.

This concerns me about our society in the United States of America today and is one of the main impetus why I am writing this book. Look at how the average person today does not want to give up any lifestyle benefits but complains about how social security will not be there for their children or doesn't care about the impact it will have on their children. Look at how the average person enjoys current lifestyle benefits but shrinks from considering the future environmental impact on their grandchildren even to the point of being "confused" about whether global warming and other issues are real.

Look at how people made huge amounts of money in the Enron scandal, Tyco, and even Arthur Anderson, and had no thought of the damage it would cause to thousands of people's retirement let alone the economy or generations of cynicism about business. This is really nothing new thought. This behavior has occurred throughout history both in nations and in families in cycles, after abundance had been received not earned. A different higher value is established when something is earned than when it is received. When life hurts bad enough the choice to move forward becomes more obvious and easier to make for the average individual.

For a compassionate samurai the immediate pain is irrelevant if it is outweighed by long-term benefits. The compassionate samurai would endure the greatest physical pain particularly when they've been wounded in battle. Despite how badly they where in physical pain the pain of them violating their codes was far more painful. At the founding of our country there were fifty-six signers to the declaration of independence. By signing that document they knew they were putting their fortunes, families and life in jeopardy for the opportunity to pursue liberty for themselves and others. They were without a doubt compassionate samurai. Because of their act of courage we now enjoy liberty. You may wonder did they too pay a price? Absolutely yes!

- Five signors were captured by the British as traitors and tortured before they died.

- Twelve had their homes ransacked and burned

- Two lost their sons serving in the Revolutionary Army another had two sons captured.

- Nine of the 56 fought and died from the wounds or hardships of the Revolutionary War.

That's just the short-listing of the high price that those men paid. Being a compassionate samurai is not a free ride through life with all benefits. There are major costs involved. We have received this liberty and now must recreate the value of the liberty or our heirs will lose it. Remember excitement builds momentum, but only character lasts.

The choice is no longer between violence and nonviolence; it is either nonviolence and nonexistence.

—*Martin Luther King, Hr., "The American Dream" speech given at Lincoln University, Oxford Pennsylvania, 6 June 1961*

Liberty is more precious than gold and silver, and requires more discipline to obtain and maintain. Dr. Myles Munroe in his book The Burden of Freedom calls Irresponsibility: Freedom's Greatest Enemy. He is using freedom the way I am using liberty. He says, "You are where you are because you have subconsciously chosen to be." That means many of our choices are made by our sub-conscious. Of irresponsibility Munroe writes:

The word irresponsibility also carries with it the meaning of "lacking conscience" or unable or unwilling to respond to conscience." It is mankind's conscience that allows us to distinguish between right and wrong. When a lifestyle of irresponsibility is allowed to increase, the voice of conscience is progressively silenced. Some people are doing unbelievable things, yet they have no sense of guilt or remorse after they've finished. People are shooting each other. Husbands are beating their wives. Fathers sleep with their daughters, wake up, shower, eat breakfast and go off to work as if nothing happened. Conscience has died throughout much of the world's society because we have inherited a spirit of irresponsibility. (The Burden of Freedom pg 57)

If what Munroe is saying is true, and I believe that it is, then we can directly correlate liberty to responsibility and bondage to irresponsibility. Isn't it true that many people in our prisons acted irresponsibly which is why they have lost their liberty? If you drive down the street at 100 miles an hour in a 45 mph zone the liberty to drive will be taken away from you. If you are disbarred because you participated in fraudulent actions as a lawyer, then you will have your privilege to practice law taken away from you.

Liberty is removed, sometimes permanently in the environment of irresponsible behavior. Liberty is lost when average people failed to act responsibly. If that is the case, then it seems like the only way to maintain one's liberty in every area of our lives is to become personally responsible for our own actions. That means you and I become true compassionate samurai. It is important to see that not all the choices, benefits, and costs are so grandiose. People deal with choices every day. The challenge of choice comes at two sets of circumstances:

a. When there are immediate benefits to the poor choice and the long-term prices are hidden.

b. When there are obvious prices to the right choice and the long-term benefits are hidden.

One of the things that we often do in our Klemmer & Associate Leadership Seminars is help people identify areas where they don't think they have choices and illuminate the choices they do have. This can be very difficult because it requires they release all the benefits of pretending they don't have choice or taking the victim viewpoint. Some of those benefits are:

Benefits of being a victim

1. Exempts you from having to take action.

2. People feel sorry for you and have pity parties for you. And that makes you feel good, wanted, accepted, and loved.

3. Victims never have to make tough decisions in life.

4. Never feel any feelings of obligations to do anything great in life, after all if "this thing" never happened to me *I* really wouldn't be this way.

5. For the rest of your life you can comfortably believe that your life's failures are directly connected to what someone else did to you and blame them.

People love to be victims because of all the benefits listed above. When you live in the place of being a victim, you never have to feel personally responsible for anything in your life. Consider Oprah Winfrey who at an early age was molested by family members more than once. She could have very easily chosen to follow the easy path of the millions of other African American young girls in the south that experienced the same trauma.

Instead she used the thing that could have crippled her to advance her cause in life of helping people. Do you believe that because she chose not to allow the rape to stop her that she is trivializing the rape? Some people believe that. They believe that if she doesn't air her pain to the world that she is somehow allowing the rapist to get of the hook. This is not about who gets off the hook or not, it's about who lives life to the fullest. It's already pretty obvious that any rapist is not living life to their optimal capacity; if they were they wouldn't have to rape people.

Oprah is in a far better position now to expose every child molester in America. She owns her own television network. If she allowed herself to become a victim, she would never have had the opportunity to be where she is now, thus limiting her influence and her widespread power to help millions become free. Choosing to not be a victim is not only about you but also about the people whom you are assigned to help get free. I know that some people would much rather be victims rather than being free because there are immediate benefits to being a victim.

Dr. Ben Carson is a noted neurosurgeon who became the director of Pediatric Neurosurgery at John Hopkins Hospital when he was only 33 years old. He is one of the most skilled pediatric neurosurgeons in the world and became very famous for his ability to separate Siamese twins in surgery, a feat that many of his peers have not been able to do successfully. But his life did not start off with great successes. He was born in Detroit to a single mother. His mother married at the age of 13 and when Carson was 8 years old his parents divorced.

She worked three and four jobs to try to provide a decent living for her sons. Although she didn't even get further than the 3rd grade, she sincerely desired that her sons Ben and his oldest brother Curtis have a better education than she did. Ben was called names and taunted by his classmates in school. They often called him "dummy" when he could not appropriately answer the questions in class. The way that he dealt with their name-calling was to vent back with uncontrollable anger fits. Even as a teenager Ben came close to killing another boy because of his uncontrollable anger. That was a life defining moment for him.

Instead of becoming a statistic he chose to educate his mind above the slurs that where being whirled at him. He began to astonish his classmates over and again with his unusual mastery of scientific knowledge. Eventually he graduated from Yale University with a degree in Psychology and then received his M.D. degree from the University of Michigan. Dr. Carson could have easily chosen to become a victim and reaped all of the benefits of doing so. He realized the same thing that true warriors realize, and that is this; there is no real enduring, long-lasting, life-improving benefit to being a victim. Being a victim keeps you right where you are.

I'm Not Your Problem

No one in life is your problem. You may say, "My mother wasn't there for me," or "my dad talked to me like I was crap." That may be, but they are not your problem. Your boss, your professor, your up line recruiter, your drill sergeant, not even your children are your problem. The whole list that I just mentioned is people, not problems. The only problems that there are in life are the ones that we appoint. Another way of looking at it is the problems in life are problems only because you haven't yet solved the problem.

I've heard of mothers blaming the fact that they had children at an early age for the reason why they couldn't go to college or pursue their career in life. They made their children their problem. Their children in fact were not their problem but rather an excuse for them to not move forward. It's

34

kind of interesting how people choose to make some things their problem while others use the same thing to advance them.

Ben Carson's mother used the fact that she had two children with no one to help her to motivate her to provide the best life and example for her sons that she could. She didn't have education but she made sure that her children would. His mother Sonya, would ask Ben and his brother to write book reviews, two each week, and turn them into her for review. After that, they would be allowed to go outside and play with the other kids. She didn't even read very well herself, and could not really assess whether the reports were written correctly or not.

None of that mattered to her. She knew that her kids were not her problem. Carson's father who walked out on his mother when he was eight was not her problem or Carson's. Either of them could have easily made him their problem. But what good would that have done? Not very much. Remember, no one is your problem. You take responsibility for everything. You are in control. You're in the drivers seat, no one else.

This Isn't A Blame Game

The blame game has to be the biggest waste of time of all games. Why? Nothing changes. To blame yourself or others is an absolute waste of time in terms of solving the problem. For the moment you just feel better. But nothing really changes. Years ago Bill Cosby made a joke in one of his standup comedy acts.

He was talking about kids who grow up as the only child and the dilemma they face, not having to blame siblings for things that they do wrong. In some ways, he was saying that having siblings gives rise to blaming. That may be true but that's not always healthy. I know from rearing children in my own experience that blaming siblings weakens a child's ability to be truly accountable for their actions in life. And surprisingly it starts off that early in life. Even at infant stage, something will occur like milk being spilled on the floor.

A parent will ask, "Who did it? A child instinctively points at someone, knowing that he has to satisfy the answer by pointing the finger at someone, even if that someone happens to be the wrong person. They are solving the problem of being pressured by giving the wrong answer. There is another way to resolve the pressure: understand that being responsible and blame have nothing to do with each other. Being personally responsible acknowledges the choices we have made and that is very different than blame.

A compassionate samurai understands that and consequently has no interest or time for blame. Imagine if I had an argument with my wife. I made more than 1,000 very conscious choices helping to set the stage for the argument. I chose to marry my wife, I chose to bring a certain topic up, I chose to bring the topic up when she was tired and had other things on her mind, and I chose to get angry at her response. Does any of that mean I am at fault for the argument? No! A compassionate samurai separates fault and blame from personal responsibility and thus is willing to take the viewpoint of being responsible for everything.

A closely related reason for not operating from responsible is held by many Christians. I see this because I am a born again believing Christian. Their paradigm of either/ or (which we will address more fully in Chapter Eight the Abundance Chapter) views the idea that either I am responsible or God is responsible. That box means that if I am going to be responsible I must deny God being all-powerful. That sounds humanistic so a fundamentalist believer would reject that. Or I let God be all-powerful and now I am victim to whatever happens as "God's will".

This is where unfortunately many Christians sit. They blame the devil or they blame God so they do not have to be responsible. In my humble opinion this is hogwash. God is all-powerful and you are responsible. It is not either or, it is a both. The way to see that is exactly what we have been talking about. It is the idea that we always have choices and yet that has nothing to do with who is at fault. Whose at fault really doesn't matter.

*"We make a living by what we get.
We make a life by what we give." —Winston Churchill.*

*Compassionate samurai give without
thought of personal gain.*

*Average people give when there is something
in it for them and it doesn't cost them too much.*

Chapter Three

Contribution

W hat is the bigger picture in life? For the compassionate samurai, the bigger picture always leads to the question, "How can I serve this person, organization or country?" In fact, the Latin meaning of samurai is "to serve." The average person is always asking, "What's in it for me?" The average businessperson leads an ordinary life. An extraordinary businessperson makes a great profit and continuously wins in the market place. But a compassionate samurai businessperson not only is highly profitable but also chooses to make a great contribution to their community, society, the people who work with and for them, and their customers.

Compassionate samurai also gives to those they will never see in this lifetime, by leaving a positive legacy. A compassionate samurai not only makes a contribution, they *are* contribution. You can only give in life that which you have. The compassionate samurai realizes that whatever they have is not solely for their own use, but for the use and benefit of others. This includes their finances, time, talents, even life itself. No matter where in life a compassionate samurai is they are looking for ways to contribute.

Sometimes there is something in it for themselves and sometimes not. At times they have lots to give and sometimes they do not. Regardless of their personal circumstance they give and are of service to others continuously. They lead a lifestyle of giving. In the year 1570 during the war for unification of Japan there was the battle of Anegawa. Two great daimio's or warlords were battling with their armies. One was Asakura Yoshilage and the other was Tokugawa Ieyasu. Asakura's army became surrounded. In order to provide time, and an opportunity for Asakura to retreat and reorganize, one of his grand champions Makara Jurozaemon offered a challenge.

A champion from Tokugawa's army accepted it. Makara won the fight, and then another champion fought him. This continued until eventually he was beat and beheaded. Makara's son stayed with him during these battles while the rest of Asakura's army retreated and reorganized. The son was beheaded also. Makara gave his life as the contribution to save the army. His son gave his life to support his father. Not only did they save the army, but also they gained honor and a legacy that exist to this day, 400 plus years later.

Compassionate samurai are willing to give their life as a contribution for a great cause or for principles. An average person values their life above all else. They are survival oriented. This is not to say a compassionate samurai is a martyr always giving to the point where they have nothing. Some people do have this martyr lifestyle. They give of their time to their children, to their job, to the community etc. and never give time to themselves.

This results in burnout where they have nothing left to give their children, job, or the community. Some people give money to their church and others, and yet never invest anything for their own accumulation. Because of that, they generally do not have large amounts to give to any cause. They are willing to give it all if the circumstance requires it. Martyrs neglect themselves under the cloak of nobility.

Giving To Oneself

What is the difference between a martyr and a compassionate samurai in terms of giving? The difference is what is at stake. Compassionate samurai take care of themselves as they lead a giving lifestyle. Giving to themselves is an okay thing. They don't feel guilty receiving. Martyrs on the other hand, often feel guilty receiving for their own purposes, thinking that it may violate their objective. Giving to oneself increases one's capacity to give. In fact it is part of the giving lifestyle. What is not okay; is when giving to oneself, is at the expense or exclusion of others.

If you give all your money away you not only live like a pauper but also have no reserves to sustain yourself or others in challenging times. If you do not give time to yourself to take care of your body, you will not have a life to give others. Don't mistake this for selfishness. This is not about selfish giving. It is an appropriate self worth that says I am worthy as are others. The life of a compassionate samurai is a life of giving. They give continuously and that also includes giving to themselves. They appreciate the high value and gift of life.

6 Benefits of Giving

Why give at all? To adopt the lifestyle of a compassionate samurai means that you will give whether it is comfortable or difficult to do so. It means to give whether you want to or not. It means to give whether there is anything in it for you or not. That can be tough for some people, so let's build a case to substantiate why you should give, so then you'll be far more willing to rise to the challenge. There are six primary benefits to giving:

1. *It feels good*

2. *Giving to get*

3. *It builds loyalty*

4. *It increases your power*

5. *Recognition*

6. *Spirituality*

The first benefit of giving is that it just plain feels good. There is nothing wrong with feeling good. Giving may not always feel good, but most frequently it does. It's actually cheaper than drugs! And, it's not illegal. Have you ever had the experience where you see a girl scout selling cookies? Walk up and for $100 you buy out an entire carton. You will smile all day long! A technique I learned from someone I consider a compassionate samurai, Bob Harrison (www.increase.org) is to carry an extra $100 bill in my wallet at all times. So whenever you feel the call, you just give the $100 bill to someone. The joy of living is in giving.

The second benefit of giving is that you get. It's a law. Not a man made law, but a law like gravity that the world operates under. It is impossible not to gain when you give. A farmer understands this. He or she gives seed and expects a harvest. Companies give to customers and they gain their business. Nordstrom was famous for it's service. They would take you all over their store, giving you first class treatment, to make sure you were taken well care of. Starbucks has gained a reputation for exceptional service where they will memorize a regular customers name and the drink they prefer. Some people get confused and expect the person they give to, to always be the one giving back to them. That is not always the case.

Your reward for giving could come back from another person or place. This is why the average person when they feel exploited by a company slacks off on what they are doing for the company thinking, "I don't get paid to handle this grief." A compassionate samurai would keep giving to the company knowing that this opens up the universe to some other company offering him or her a better job with higher pay. People give to politicians knowing that they will most likely garner favor. This type of giving however is not really giving, but trading. You offer a resource and expect something in return.

The third benefit received from giving is loyalty. If as a supervisor you are giving to a subordinate opportunity, protection, mentoring, etc. then they will most likely be very loyal to you. When you give to someone they instinctively believe that they owe you something, and that something is usually their loyalty. The fourth benefit received from giving is power. You especially gain power if you give in secret and no one knows. If you give and people know it was you that gave, you gain recognition. For an interesting review of this concept, read the book or watch the movie *The Magnificent Obsession* by Lloyd C. Douglas. The movie version of the book stars Douglas Sirk, Rock Hudson, and Jane Wyman.

A man or woman demonstrates their power not in how much they
accumulate but in how much they give.

When you give without getting any recognition something supernatural occurs where you gain power or influence that is not explainable. A man or woman demonstrates their power not in how much they accumulate but in how much they give. Contribution is actually self-serving. It however is almost counter-intuitive. Most of us grow up thinking we live in a tough dog-eat-dog world and that if you don't take care of #1, no one else will. That concept however is a myopic short-term philosophy.

The more I look out for me alone, the more everyone around me does the same, and then I find myself living in a competitive world versus a cooperative world that builds additional possibilities. The sixth benefit is spirituality. Look at anyone of almost any faith that you consider spiritual. They are a giver. Giving rejects the spirit of this world (mammon) and reaffirms God's spirit. This is why tithing is such a great practice. On a repeated emotional level as you give away the first tenth of everything you earn, you are making a statement that money does not control you.

If you give to where you receive your spiritual nourishment you are affirming how important that spiritual nourishment actually means to you. The average person is gripped by scarcity and believes they are the source of things and consequently feel that as they give away they have less. Even if you did not believe in this spiritual aspect it would still increase your prosperity. All the above benefits are gained by anyone that gives.

Here is a key distinction between the average man or woman and the compassionate samurai. Average people are not big givers and when they do give, one of the above benefits is their primary motive. Compassionate samurai think "service before self." It is a good thing to give. It is an even greater thing when the motive behind your giving is selfless. Compassionate samurai frequently give without any thought of return. There is nothing wrong when a person gives and expects something in return.

That is simply the law of sowing and reaping at work. A far greater concept is to give without the thought of where your harvest will come from. It's somewhat like the concept of agape love. God gives to us all unconditionally, whether we give back to Him or not. The challenge here is to think about contribution on a totally new level. It's easy to give more to the customer that gives the most to you. After all, one hand washes the other, right? The average person tends to have a what's in it for me mindset.

They will not give unless there is something in it for them. A compassionate samurai knows they will get back. But it is not why they give. Compassionate samurai consider it an honor and a privilege "to serve". It is their reason for being. They recognize the connectedness of all human beings and are committed to making a difference for others. They realize that their body is not who they are. They have a body, but that does not define them. Consequently, they are interested in a bigger picture that involves all of humanity.

Give Them What They Want, Not What You Want To Give Them

When average people think about giving to others there is an automatic screen that goes up. That screen, screens out all of the things that they don't really want to give, and promptly has them give what they like to give and have plenty of. What is best to give in your eyes is not always what is best in the eyes of the person that you are giving to. Giving is giving what's wanted and needed, not what I want to give. It's just human nature that we tend to give people what we think they need, rather than what they are crying out for.

In some ways, that can be a very arrogant, egotistical thing. Our ego tells us pretty regularly that we always know what someone else needs most. One of the most basic ways to find out what a person, a community, a church, or your clients needs is by simply asking them! Really. Many times it's that simple. In our seminars I have heard thousands of husbands work hard and provide a beautiful house, clothes, and great lifestyle for their wife. When you listen to the wife however, she would gladly take a bit smaller house or not go on an exotic vacation if she could have had the husband at a few more of the children's sports games or music recitals.

Many a wife has taken great care of the children, taken great care of the house, and yet the husband would rather have had the living room unkempt, or eaten a few more take out meals if the wife had more energy to be intimate at the end of the day. I am not attempting to stereotype roles here. The point is that we often give others what we think they need without ever asking what it is they really want. Sometimes at work we work hard doing what we like but it is not what is adding value to the company.

All their hard work really isn't of service, because it is not what they want. Have you ever just simply asked what your boss would like you to handle? How long has it been since you have asked your spouse or child what you can do for them? I can remember a time when my son Kelly and I were on a father and son vacation in Hawaii. I had planned out fishing trips and all kinds of activities. Then I stopped myself and practiced this art of a compassionate samurai of simply asking him what he wanted to do if he could do anything.

He replied that what he really wanted to do was watch action movies that his mother was not fond of him watching. I decided for one day on vacation that would be fine and for the next 9 hours we watched back-to-back action movies. We even brought pizza in and didn't even leave the room. To this day it is one of his favorite memories of us sharing time together. He wanted time together with me in a certain way. He did not want my advice or what I thought would be fun. I not only got a great time with him, but he then listened to me in a different way.

Sometimes people may ask you to do something you don't like doing or find uncomfortable. Thirty years ago I attended a men's seminar with my mentor, Tom. I even helped him design parts of the seminar. During one of the segments I did not design, he had us filling in dirt holes on his ranch for several days. We had all paid $7500 so you can imagine some of the reactions from the men. In addition, we knew that at the first rain the potholes would simply reappear. In our minds, the road needed to be paved with some type of blacktop, not just filled in with loose dirt. But what we wanted and how we thought it should be did not really matter. What mattered was serving my mentor, and giving him what he wanted, whether I understood his logic or not.

It took me some time to come to the realization that service is giving what's wanted, not what I want to give. That lesson has served me well over the years and is the mark of a compassionate samurai. You don't even have to know the meaning or value of what you are doing. What you need to know is that it matters to the other person. That's what contribution is about. Practice asking your boss what is it they really want. Practice with your children.

Practice with someone you date. Practice with a total stranger. You will find that some people don't know what they want. Some people are embarrassed to tell you what they want. Others may be suspicious of why you want to know; thinking you might take advantage of them with the knowledge. Learning to converse in such a way that people open up to you with what they want is something that a compassionate samurai is an expert at. Expert status doesn't come overnight, but with repeated practice. So start asking now.

Five reasons why people don't give

There are five primary reasons people do not give:

- A belief of scarcity-that there is not enough
- Self centered

- Feel that the people that they would give to don't deserve it

- Think they've already given

- Ego that says that type of giving is really beneath them

Either or Mentality

One thing that often hinders our ability to be life-long contributors and people of lasting significance is what my good friend Bob "Doctor Increase" Harrison calls the either or mindset. Either or mindset is at the very heart of scarcity and a disease of the average man or woman. One of the most obvious areas this can be seen is money. People get conditioned or programmed to believe that they must either be spiritual or have money, but not both. Another "either or" around money is they can have either money or values, but not both. They can have "money or a kind heart," but not both.

In essence this belief is that there is a fixed amount of money available and I can either take care of myself or take care of others, but not both. People that have this mindset might say, "I can either be successful in my job or in my family but not both." Either you are right or I am right, but one of us has to be wrong. There is time to do this or time to do that, but not enough time to do them both. Scarcity thinking suggests you have to make a clear-cut decision between one and the other because there is not enough to go around in this world.

A compassionate samurai knows they are enough since they are not the source
and they operate from the position of knowing that there is plenty of everything.

Scarcity thinking says there is not enough money, not enough love, not enough time, not enough good men or women, not enough good opportunities, not enough prospects or customers or anything else. That train of thought is usually based on the belief that they are not enough. A compassionate samurai knows they are enough since they are not the source and they operate from the position of knowing that there is plenty of everything. (see Chapter Eight on Abundance) This is why they always attract to themselves the people, resources and opportunities they need.

Most people have a core belief that the more they give away the less they have. This is known as fixed pie thinking. Fixed pie thinking says that there is a fixed amount of something; like a pie. Every piece you give away means there is less pie. Some games are like that. Price is one such game. Service, however, is infinite. There are an infinite number of ways you can give or contribute. Another issue at the heart of either or and scarcity is self-centeredness. The problem begins with what we think is reality and who we think we are.

People explore these questions in our seminars and they are explored, in some detail, in my books "If How To's Were Enough We Would All Be Skinny Rich and Happy" and "When Good Intentions Run Smack Into Reality." The problem begins with the fact that we believe our eyes, ears, and physical senses define reality. I look at my body and it appears male. I look at my wife's body and it appears female. To the eye it looks like I am the more outgoing type and she is shyer. Perhaps I am on a trip and it looks at the moment as if her body is in California and mine is in Australia.

From the looks of it, it appears that we are separate so then we begin to think that we are our bodies. Here's the truth, you are not your body. You just have a body. That is a BIG difference. The average person thinks they are the body and in taking care of that body they become self-centered. When you realize that you only have a body, and that in a realm that cannot see you connected to other people, you then become service oriented. When companies hire us to train their staff to do teamwork, they sometimes think we are going to do a "bonding" experience like rafting a river.

There is nothing wrong with that, except that if teamwork is based on that type of chemistry, then when the players change, the bond breaks. In business, players change all the time, so we can't use that as the standard. When people change the paradigm of who they are then they can connect with other team players regardless of who is on the team.

Another reason that prevents people from being huge givers is that they don't feel that other people are worthy of the gift. This presupposes there is some great balance we are trying to maintain, somewhat like the scales of justice. A compassionate samurai is not about justice they are about mercy. Justice is receiving what you deserve. Mercy is receiving what you don't deserve.

The fourth condition that limits people's giving is that they feel like they have already given. It is based on an assumption that a certain amount is enough or that I am not capable of giving more than so much. It's like meeting a quota for the year or month. A compassionate samurai realizes that the needs are infinite and because I am not the source there is an infinite amount to give.

Never Too Good To Be Involved

A compassionate samurai sometimes gets involved in giving on many different levels. Why? Because they are interested in fulfilling what is wanted not in protecting their image. A compassionate samurai does not have an ego problem around being of service. They realize more than anyone that if they have a high or lofty position in life it is directly connected to their ability to serve people. Microsoft, Wal-Mart, Home Depot, and Sears all became major players because they established a precedent of serving people. That is one of the reasons why their companies grew to such massive sizes.

Beyond financial gains, many of these business warriors realized that they too have to be service oriented even on a personal level. That is why you'll find some of the most successful people in the world often offer their personal time to humanity. They don't just offer their financial resources; they give of their personal time and heart. If you are a compassionate samurai CEO of a major corporation, it is nothing for you to be a CEO during the week and then help clean up a low-income inner city neighborhood on your weekend time.

Bill Gates spends his time helping African children fight against the war on aids that is destroying their communities. Former president Jimmy Carter is doing the same with helping sickened children in African villages have hope again. Oprah Winfrey is mom to more than 50,000 children in South Africa, building educational centers, hospitals, and housing for their underprivileged families. Grammy winning rock star Bono has committed the rest of his life to humanitarian efforts. Nothing is beneath them. In fact it is an honor for them to serve. That is a significant trait of a compassionate samurai.

There was a time when my mentor was hosting a seminar and the owner of a very large restaurant chain was a volunteer on staff. Tom, my mentor, made a comment about the trash needing to be taken out. Bob, the restaurant owner, immediately took the trash out and in fact he took it one step further, and washed the trash can! My mentor joked later that if he hadn't stopped him, he probably would have painted it gold. Bob was not concerned with ego. Taking the trash out was not beneath him. He heard a need and he handled it and took his same attitude of excellence to a very mundane task. That's service. That's giving what is wanted and not what we want to give.

Giving What You Have Very Little Of

A compassionate samurai's power is demonstrated by what he or she gives, not by what they accumulate. Give of what you have very little of, not just what you have in abundance. Average people give what they already have plenty of. People that don't have a lot of money will sometimes say, "I will give my time or talent," as if that excuses them from giving money. They are ruled by their scarcity. If what is needed is hard for you, it is all the more reason for you to give that. Look at it as a set of weights for you to work out with. The more you give what is hard the bigger the muscles you will build in that area.

Giving changes the giver as much as it changes the recipient.

You will increase your capacity to give. How do you get more of what you want? You sow that same commodity. If you are pressed for time then you give some of your time away. Some successful people tend to have very little time to do humanitarian efforts. Because of that they tend to shrink back from those types of service, which includes their personal involvement and just write checks instead. That does not equate to their fullest contribution. They need to give what they have little of in addition to what they have much of. Giving changes the giver as much as it changes the recipient.

If you have a hardened heart, then give some of your heart away. Giving access to you, your vulnerability, or friendship are amazing enabling gifts. Sometimes receiving is the best gift you can give. Receiving certainly requires greater vulnerability than traditional giving. When my dad allows me to give to him it is the greatest gift he can give me. He doesn't need anything, but allowing me to give to him is a gift to me. As a child he has given me so much over the years, that now I just want to give back to him. Some parents, due to their association of receiving as being a weakness, don't allow their children to give to them and that's really a shame.

Giving Up To Go Up

Each economic class has a different challenge around giving. If we generalized, I'd say the middle class is in a comfort zone. Mediocrity is a selfish pursuit. If we are not striving for more because we are comfortable then we care more about our own condition than we do the condition of others. Our comfort has taken precedence over our ability to contribute. If you see a starving child, yet do not have the ability to provide food, then all you can do is feel for them. This is the state of the average man or woman.

A compassionate samurai is constantly increasing their capacity to give so they can give. Perhaps you have heard the phrase, "be ye hot or be ye cold, but the lukewarm He shall spew out of His mouth." Perhaps God would rather us be hotter than be indifferent or mediocre. Robert Kiyosaki and Donald Trump in their book, <u>Why We Want You To Be Rich</u>, deals quite extensively on the major fallout within the next decade amongst the middle class of America. They suggest there will be two classes in America, either the poor or the rich.

They also suggest that either side is a matter of choice, and your choice to educate yourself to the language of finance, or to ignore it. The poor will remain poor unless they get a revelation of their own God given potential and realize they do not have to be poor nor is it spiritually noble. The rich are already rich because they have applied and mastered the science of wealth. They understand the laws that govern wealth and how to use their creativity to create a fortune. The struggle of the wealthy is for what purpose?

As a compassionate samurai they use money as a vehicle to contribute and make a difference and it affects the fulfillment in their life. It is not the end but only a means. Some people hold so tightly onto their dollars because they feel that money is their security. Others hold onto their money tightly because they are afraid they will become poor again. And some believe hoarding their money is the way to riches. This is not to say middle class people don't give.

A good leader always replaces himself or herself with someone who is better.

An interesting statistic on giving in the USA annual report of 2000 is that 200 billion dollars was given to not for profit organizations. 5% came from corporations, 7% from foundations and 88% from individuals. Of the amount from individuals 75% came from those earning less than $150,000 a year.

Sometimes we have to give up control in order to grow an organization. At times we may have to give up being the star and let someone else get the recognition for us to move up into management. Giving does not mean you are losing anything although that's the way the average person sees it. A good leader always replaces himself or herself with someone who is better. One of the things they give is their knowledge and training. Average people hoard their knowledge so that they are the only ones who know how to do something and in the process lose their job.

"Tell me to what you pay attention to and I will tell you who you are." —Jose Ortega Y Gasset.

Compassionate samurai anchor reality to their vision .

Average people anchor their vision to reality.

Chapter Four

Focus

Focus is the ability to direct one's attention, efforts, or activity at a desired direction or object without being distracted. A compassionate samurai can choose to focus on anything and then maintain that focus. Average people neither select a focus nor are they able to maintain it. The amazing attribute of focus is leverage. Focus leverages average talent, small amounts of time, or minimal resources into extraordinary results. It is the fulcrum to a lever. Without a doubt it is a quality that makes or breaks a compassionate samurai. It is also the deciding factor of whether or not a samurai will ever achieve greatness in life.

Focus leverages power. A magnifying glass focuses the power of the sun. The same amount of energy is there with or without a magnifying glass. With a magnifying glass it can light a fire. A laser will cut through six inches of steel with the same amount of energy that goes through a 75-watt light bulb. It is focused rather than diffused. In my book If How To's Were Enough We Would All Be Skinny Rich and Happy, we introduced a model of us as human beings with three levels.

The three levels were the conscious mind or head, the subconscious mind or heart, and an infinite level I call God. Your conscious mind is the place where choice, and thus focus resides. It is important that the magnifying glass does not get confused and thinks it is the power or the sun. Your conscious mind is the magnifying glass, your subconscious is the manufacturing plant, and God is the source. A compassionate samurai can remain humble amidst doing great things recognizing that he or she is merely the magnifying glass.

The three challenges of focus that average people succumb to:

1. They are not focused either due to an unwillingness or inability to focus

2. They are focused on things that make them ineffective

3. Often they are focused but still unaware and blind to things that surround them

Let's deal with people's unwillingness or inability to focus. Life is full of distractions and few people really focus. Ask people "What is the purpose of your life?" A vast majority of people will stutter, stammer, and say they just don't know. Their life is unfocused. Ask most people during breakfast what are the three things you are absolutely going to accomplish today and they can't tell you. They are just going to work hard, and handle what comes up, whatever that is. They are unfocused. Ask most husbands and wives what is the focus of your marriage and you will most likely be greeted with a blank stare.

One reason average people don't learn to focus is that they live under the false assumption that focus will require great amounts of effort and be a strain on them in some way or another. Most people, in fact, are either, focused and uptight or having fun and unfocused. This relates to their scarcity thinking of "either or" covered in the previous chapter. A compassionate samurai is better able to make wise decisions, think clearly and has fun all at the same time, when they are focused and relaxed

Many years ago, my mentor Tom held a ten-day men's workshop. There were approximately 40 men on a ranch. These men came from all walks of life. Some were considered by the world to be very successful and some were considered not so successful, although all of still had paid $7500.00 to participate. At one point, without explaining anything to us, Tom asked us all to pull $100.00 out of our wallet. I was close to my mentor and although I had no idea what he was up to, I did know for sure he was going to demonstrate a valuable lesson that we could live by.

That was his very nature. After he asked us to pull out the money, I saw many different kinds of reactions. Some of the guys just didn't want to do it at all. They were suspicious that they were going to lose their money. Others were frustrated because they didn't have that much in their wallet. Some of the guys boastfully pulled out their money, mistakenly thinking that their net worth was parallel to their self worth. Others were simply curious as to what Tom was up to. After all the men pulled out their money, Tom pulled out a rifle.

He then explained the rules to the game. The men had just entered a competition. They had paid $100.00 to enter. Each man would get one minute to fire five rounds at a target downfield. The best score would take ALL the money, approximately $4,000.00. I remembered thinking this is good because I am an ex-military man and have fired a rifle many times whereas many of the other men had never fired a weapon in their life. I felt I had a chance to win at Tom's game. The first gentleman stood up to fire and just as he was about to squeeze the trigger Tom began screaming in his ear.

The gentleman jerked the rifle as he fired missing the target wildly. Tom laughed and said with only four bullets and 40 seconds left he might as well give up. He would never win. The gentleman was stunned and without any resistance simply put the rifle down, and gave up. The next man stood up. Before firing he looked over at Tom. Tom smiled. The man turned back to fire and again just as he was about to fire, Tom started screaming like a wild man. This went on until every man had taken his turn.

You can bet that we all screamed loudly in Tom's ears when it was his turn. Finally, we compared all the targets. I had come in second. Not bad, but no money for a prize. Tom had come in first with the best score. Incredibly, most people just wandered off feeling a bit jaded and swindled out of their money. I asked Tom what the lesson was in all this, because although I couldn't see the lesson I knew he always had one. Tom asked me a simple question. "Are there distractions in life?" The answer to that was easy-of course, there are many.

Then he asked another simple question. "Are there money and time pressures in life?" Again I replied yes, still struggling to see the point. He then explained that the game mirrored life. His yelling in our ears simulated the distractions in our life. We have phone calls disrupting our planned day, work that interferes with our relationships and problems in relationships that interferes with work. Challenges with kids distract us from romance in a marriage. A serious illness interrupts our planned life. *Life is full of distractions.*

The potential loss of our $100 and the potential gain of $4,000 simulated the money pressures of life. In the physical world we live in, people can downplay this, but *money pressure exists.* It costs money to rent or buy a house. Good schools and higher education cost money. Groceries cost money, let alone trying to fit in with the right clothes or late model car. Limited to one minute for all five shots simulated the *time pressure* we are under. You have a conversation with your son or daughter yet you don't have all day to get it right. There is only a certain amount of time, after that you lose patience and are on with your life.

You make a sales call or have a management meeting and even with incomplete information you have a limited amount of time to get the job done or to make the right decision. Time and money pressure are a part of life. They aren't going anywhere. In case you have never fired a weapon here is a pointer for you. If you focus on a target, but get uptight you'll miss the target. If you relax yet are unfocused you still miss the target.

At West Point they would scream in your face while you had to recite various things you were required to memorize. Although I didn't understand what they were trying to teach me at the time, I was learning to be relaxed and focused at the same time. That rigorous training is what caused me to come in second place in Tom's little game. He was just better at it than I was. No matter how many distractions come our way, or how much financial pressure or time pressure we have in life, if we have concentrated focus and stay relaxed we will hit the bull's eye every time. That's one of the practices of a compassionate samurai. That is one of the reasons I love the game of golf. I can practice being relaxed and focused.

When I am relaxed and focused, the ball goes much further and way more accurate than when I tighten up and try and hit the ball with great force. It is almost counter intuitive. Let the club do the work. One of my good friends is a gentleman named Doug Firebaugh. He is considered a guru and outstanding trainer in the home based, network-marketing industry because of the results he has produced and the tens of thousands of people he has helped (www.passionfire.com).

Every Christmas he does training for those in that industry that addresses the fact that for the majority of people, their network marketing business slows down during the holidays and yet it should accelerate since everybody is in the buying mood. The average person relaxes with the holidays and becomes unfocused. He walks people through how they can relax and yet be focused and significantly increase their business with ease. He uses the very same principle, and it works.

Focusing On Ineffective Things

What is the point of you living? Why are you here on earth? Knowing the answer to those questions is having focus for your life. These are important questions for you to grapple with if you are to have focus. Then it is a matter of not allowing the many distractions of life to sway you from your purpose. *A compassionate samurai has a focus of service or contribution no matter what circumstances he or she is in.* Average people focus on themselves and really don't care what happens to others. How much money can I make? How good can I feel in a relationship? How good do I look?

A compassionate samurai has a focus of service or contribution
no matter what circumstances he or she is in.

In the event that average people consider others, it is only to insure that they have more, feel better, and are ahead of the pack. Some of the greatest leaders of our time endured unusual pressure such as Mahatma Gandhi, Martin Luther King jr., Nelson Mandela, Mother Theresa and many others. What these compassionate samurai had in common is that each of them continued to focus on their vision for a better world for everyone. They never wavered to the left or right. They stayed grounded and centered on their focus regardless of many incredible pressures.

Torture, having their families lives threatened, periodically being without money to fund their projects, and public ridicule were just a few of the pressures they endured. That is one of the amazing things about a compassionate samurai is that no matter what is going on around them they stay true to their focus. They know that even the slightest distraction could cost many others their destinies. Some people try and get themselves off the hook by thinking this level of focus only happens in a grandiose fashion with special people. You too can be a compassionate samurai.

One of the ways a compassionate samurai stays focused is to keep death in his or her mind all the time. Before you get caught in thinking this is a morbid preoccupation, work this line of thinking through. A compassionate samurai lives every day as if it might be their last day so they live life to the fullest, playing full out. Confronting one's death alleviates the fear of death and lends clarity of purpose to what life is about. Average people pretend they have at least 75 years to live and dilute the intensity of their life.

In Thomas Cleary's book, The Code of the Samurai: A Modern Translation of the Bushido Shoshinshu of Tiara Shigesuke, he writes:

One who is supposed to be a warrior considers it his foremost concern to keep death in mind at all times, every day and every night, from the morning of New Year's Day through the night of New Year's Eve. As long as you keep death in mind at all times, you will also fulfill the ways of loyalty and familial duty. You will also avoid myriad evils and calamities, you will be physically sound and healthy, and you will live a long life. What is more, your character will improve and your virtue will grow. (pg 3)

Clearly continues....

When you assume that your stay in this world will last, various wishes occur to you, and you become very desirous. You want what others have, and cling to your own possessions, developing a mercantile mentality. (pg 5)

Clearly suggests that keeping death in mind is the treatment for covetousness and greed, among a host of other evils. The purpose here is not to get you to run out and pick out your favorite casket and tombstone. Rather, it is to live your life with a sense of purpose and urgency. If today were the last day of your life, how would you spend it? Who would you be a blessing to? What kind of support system would you set up for your loved one's left behind? Perhaps you would talk to an old friend, or tell someone that you loved him or her.

If today were the last day of your life, how would you spend it?

Maybe you would seek out a spiritual experience that you've always dreamed of. Whatever the case may be, you would live your life free of the mundane affairs of everyday life that have proven to be little more than distractions adding very little value if any at all. When you live with death in mind, you are not trying to protect life and simply survive because you know it is a lost cause. You play full out because you don't have life to lose.

Forgetting—The Key To Focusing On The Effective Things

I am writing this section on an airplane after conducting one of our one evening Champions Workshops to a group in Detroit. Someone came up to me at the end of the session and passionately explained how bad they wanted to attend our weekend workshop called Personal Mastery, but they just couldn't afford it. I asked, "What ideas have you come up with to create any money?" Her response was, "none." Notice that she was passionate and had lots of energy. What was her problem? She had her focus in the wrong direction. She was focused on her problem and not on a solution.

This woman's problem in this case was that she had no money. That was a condition of her past. She needed to forget her problem and her past. With zero focus on a working solution, it was no wonder she had zero answers. Average people ask the question "Can I?" They base their answer on their past. Compassionate samurai ask a different question. They ask, "How can I?" Even if no more energy is applied, because it has a different focus, it has enormously different results. Try that out in your own life. Pick something that you decided you couldn't do for whatever reason.

You didn't have the time, you didn't have the money, or you couldn't get a babysitter. Perhaps it was buying a house, or losing 20 pounds, maybe even getting a new job. What is it? Write it down. Commit now to spending an hour solving that problem. What was your experience? If you are an average reader you just blew by that last sentence and are waiting for me to tell you what your experience most likely was. Do yourself a favor and put down this book and spend an hour solving whatever problem you decided you couldn't solve.

Compassionate samurai don't get to their level by just reading alone. Samurai are "take action" kind of people. You have to fight some battles. You have to spend the time training. Consider this part of your training in learning to focus. Now what was your experience? Was there a level of resistance in even doing it? That is an inability to focus. A compassionate samurai can make a decision to focus on anything and then is able to maintain that focus.

In our weekend seminar called *Personal Mastery* we have people practice the art and skill of focusing. It is not just a matter of being focused or not focused. We try to get people to realize what they are focusing on.

There is an exercise I used to do where people break one-inch thick boards with their bare hand. Their ability to break the boards is not a matter of muscle, but rather of concentrated focus. The very first time we did that exercise, my wife was adamant against doing it. That would have been fine since in our seminars everything is one's personal choice. The focus is on "learning" and many times people will learn as much or even more by not doing any exercise. In this case, my wife saw a petite oriental female 13-year-old break the board.

She recognized that it was not a matter of strength and mustered up the courage and broke her own board. We put the broken board in a very nice frame in our home. Every time she looks at the board, it triggers her to "focus" and to appreciate how powerful she is when focused. One of the immediate things that occurred as a result of that in her life, is she headed up a spaghetti dinner fund raiser for the Parent Teachers Association of one of our children's school. Up until that point she had always been a volunteer, but never willing to be responsible for being the head.

By forgetting her past image of herself she produced the largest fund raising dinner up until that time for that PTA. Focus can overcome incredible odds by developing odds of its own. Tiger Woods is one of, if not the best golfer alive today. It might even be argued that he is perhaps the best golfer of all time. One of his skills that make him a compassionate samurai is his ability to forget. I have seen him strike a ball off the fairway into the woods. On his very next shot he will incredibly make the green.

An average person would be beating themselves up over the next 10 strokes and ruin their score by compounding the problem. Tiger is able to quickly forget and hit each shot as a fresh start. This idea applies in all areas of life. Can you forget the fact your spouse forgot it was you anniversary and didn't get you a card let alone a gift? If so, you can have an incredible marriage. The average person cannot forget. They focus on the problem. What is the worst thing you have ever done? Can you forget it? If you can't forget it, can you at least attach no meaning to it so that it becomes neutral and doesn't affect your life?

A compassionate samurai can forget. I have seen thousands of people who allow their past to plague their future. It may have been years after a certain tragic thing occurred in a person's life, and they just can't seem to let that thing go. They allow the negativity of their painful past to become their every day reality. As long as you allow your past to haunt you, you will never be free to focus on your future. You won't even be able to focus on what is going on right now.

Compassionate samurai forget their successes as well as their failures!

Are you familiar with Paul in the Bible? Regardless of your religious persuasion it is a great example of forgetting. He wrote more than 2/3 of the New Testament. He was educated under the tutelage of Gamaliel, a law professor, graduating with high honors and distinctions. Yet this genius, readily confesses he doesn't know it all. That's a salient point. *Compassionate samurai*

forget their successes as well as their failures! The average person holds onto their successes and forfeits even more spectacular success.

Never let your good get in the way of your spectacular. Paul also had a terrible past of persecuting followers of Christ, torturing and even beheading some. How could he become a crusader for the cause of Christ with such a tainted past? There was only one way—to forget. Forgetting frees us to focus on something new. A compassionate samurai never lets what matters most to suffer for the things that matter least. That which matters most is where a compassionate samurai concentrates their focus. Suffering is optional, although pain is not. **Suffering is the unnecessary prolongation of a painful experience by remaining focused on the pain.**

Be Here Now

There is an old concept that we teach in our Personal Mastery Seminars related to focus called, "Be Here Now." This concept means that your body, feelings, spirit, and thoughts are all at the same place at the same time. Have you ever been physically home, but your mind was still at work? That's not being here now. Have you ever done a job and you're your heart was not into it? That's not being here now. *When a person is not being here now, effectiveness and intimacy are killed.* The average person is not mentally disciplined to be here now.

When a person is not being here now, effectiveness and intimacy are killed.

When they have a problem they keep focusing on the problem instead of being here now and creating a solution. Have you ever seen a deer frozen in headlights? Often the car hits the deer. The deer was focused on the wrong thing, the headlights. It became distracted from the here and now concept. That's the story of the average person's life. The deer could easily outrun and out maneuver the car. By focusing on the wrong thing the deer lost her ability and got paralyzed by circumstances. A compassionate samurai never allows circumstances to impair their vision on focusing on what is important.

Focused But Not Blinded

Some people use as an excuse not to focus that they would "miss out" on too many other things. Have you ever heard or known of someone that is so focused on their work that they ignore their family? Of course you have. However this is confusing two concepts and is an outgrowth of the scarcity and "either or" mentalities. First of all, *a Compassionate Samurai is both focused and has 360 degrees awareness at the same time.* That is a skill to develop. In Aikido someone can throw a punch at you and you are very focused on responding to that punch, but at the same time you must be aware of what is going on behind you. Although two things are happening, it is still considered singularity of focus.

It's very possible that there maybe a threat there. Are other people in the vicinity or not? Are they friendly or not? I am known in my family and at work for my strong ability to focus. My ability to maintain 360-degree awareness is something I have had to work on and at times has been pretty humorous. I will focus on driving and my children could pass by on the opposite side of the road in their car, wave at me and I will never see them. Perhaps the funniest time was one October I came home on a red eye "all night" plane trip and then drove home from the airport.

When I arrived there it was about 7:00 A.M., and I joined my wife and daughter shortly before my daughter went off to school. Roma asked me if I wanted an early Christmas present. I said, "no I would rather wait'. She giggled that we might have a problem. My daughter started to laugh. I didn't get what was going on and Roma told me to go back in the living room. I did, and to my surprise there was a huge 54-inch wide screen color television with a bow wrapped around it.

The strange thing is that I had passed through the living room at least three times drinking a cup of coffee and thinking. I was so focused on my thoughts I had never seen the television. How can you miss a 54-inch TV? By being focused on something else. When my family wants to have fun with me they tease me by calling me the "King of Awareness". What 54-inch TV opportunities have you missed because you were not focused or were focused but then lacked an awareness of what was going on around you?

Many men have been so focused on their professional life and have lacked the 360-degree awareness, being blind to family problems developing. The key is not to be driven by scarcity and go "either or" but to do both. You can do both at the same time. In the beginning you may have to practice simply focusing on what is in front of you and then switching. This is being able to focus on work while at work and then focusing on home while at home. It is focusing on one problem at work with one manager and then ten minutes later you have taken all your thought and focused it on a totally different issue with a different person.

The speed with which you can shift your focus is an ability you want to spend time developing. It will effectively mobilize your power and creativity, but it is still only one step on the way to being focused and having 360-degree awareness simultaneously. The next conversation you have with someone, focus on his or her words. That alone is VERY difficult for most people. Most people are so focused on what they want to say and are anxiously looking for an opening to say it, that they don't really hear what the other person is saying.

Or they may be distracted by a family crisis and are thinking about that as the other person is talking. As you learn to be focused on "what they are saying" learn to increase your 360 degree awareness. You will become aware of not just the words they are saying but whatever they are feeling. You will be able to feel what they are not saying, that is important. You will become aware of what is going on for the person sitting next to the person you are talking to and they haven't even said anything. You will become aware of the overall energy in the room.

*Compassionate samurai say what they mean
and mean what they say.*

Average people are honest when it's convenient.

*"I hope I shall possess firmness and virtue enough to
maintain what I consider the most enviable of all titles,
the character of an honest man." —George Washington*

Chapter Five

Honesty

If you took a random survey of a thousand people, and asked them, "Do you think you are honest," you can be guaranteed that the vast majority of the people would answer, "Why of course I'm honest." Most people really think that they are honest. If you ask a crook is he or she honest, they'd say yes. They'd probably say, "I tell people that I am going to steal from them and that's being honest." As crazy as it may sound, that is how some people think. People have filters in their mind concerning honesty.

The average person's favorite saying is, "Yeah I'm honest, but." Remember, it is always the "but" that houses the lie that you are living and covering up. Genuine honesty is not covered up or watered down. There really are no ifs, ands, or buts about it. The truth is the truth. No contingencies here. Since most people have become so desensitized to dishonesty, they do not really know how to recognize when they are being dishonest.

We have established our own set of rules concerning what is honest from what is not that when we are confronted with a situation involving our own selves we escape the truth on a prefabricated "exception clause" that we've become comfortable using. "I'm honest, but taxes are another issue." That's just one of millions of lies that we tell that we feel comfortable with. When

I went to West Point, they have an honor code where if you lie, cheat, or steal or *tolerate anyone who does*, the cadets throw you out of West Point. That was pretty straightforward talk and I knew they weren't joking.

You can tell the truth and still not be honest.

Because I didn't want to get kicked out, I didn't lie, cheat, or steal while I was there, so I really thought that I was honest. It was later in life that I had to realize that I needed to check myself in the area of honesty. *You can tell the truth and still not be honest.* Honesty is really not about successfully passing an incident or two. Honesty is really about a lifestyle. It's not something that you do once in a while, it's really who you are. The compassionate samurai is honest not only when it is convenient for him or her to be so, but is honest at all times, even if it cost their life or when no one is around.

The Acceptable Lie

Once in a seminar with my mentor, Tom had us mill around the room telling people what really mattered to us that we wanted to achieve. I told people that I wanted to be more organized at work. I did want that. I wasn't directly lying, but I wasn't being totally honest. What really mattered to me was that I wanted a wildly romantic long lasting relationship. But there was no way that I was going to say that to strangers, much less people I knew. People thought I had it together and I was afraid of what they might think if I said that.

Being organized was a more acceptable response. I began to see that although I would not lie, there were plenty of places in business and personal relationships where I didn't disclose the full truth. There are many ways a lack of honesty can show up. One can become accustomed to telling people that which they think they want to hear. When a person does this, they are really hiding. They are not only hiding the total truth, but they are also hiding a piece of themselves that they really don't want others to know about them. It's the side that so few people want to reveal to others. It could be motivated by fear, or maybe even pride.

Whatever the motivation might be, some people use words, persuasive words, to cover up the real issue. Although they don't feel like they are being dishonest, they are. For the compassionate samurai, honesty is not about giving people that which they want to hear, or even that which sounds acceptable, but rather giving people the truth, the whole truth, and nothing but the truth. When people hide their truest intention and always tell people what they want them to hear, not only does it do a disservice to the person that says it, but also to the listener.

The Many Faces of Lying

Dishonesty shows up in many different ways. Just because a person tells the truth under favorable conditions doesn't mean they are lie-proof. There are some things that people tend to do, that they don't even realize is actually being dishonest. This section is not just about exposing your lies. This section is far more about revelation, in the sense of self-discovery. There are some things that you may not know about yourself that once revealed might give you a clearer light on you. So the ways listed here are more about helping you to understand some of the ways that you can make a more gallant effort in being honest, even in unfavorable conditions.

There are several ways to be dishonest:

1. **Telling somebody something that is not so.** This is the most obvious way to be dishonest. Perhaps you have heard stories of where in the Vietnam War, body counts were highly inflated to give information that upper management wanted. The person telling the lie knows it is incorrect. Managers will tell a boss they will make something happen and they know they can't. Sales people promise results, (unrealistic) just to make a sale. People do this to make themselves look good, be accepted, and avoid negative consequences or to get people off their back.

2. **Giving the illusion of what is not so.** People whose job it is to make cold calls to sell services might say, "I made 20 calls." In reality, they only talked to 10 people and left 10 messages. They know that talking to ten people represents their reality and the amount of people that they called in actuality. In theory they can call one thousand people and talk with no one. So really they've called no one. They've given the illusion of having done something that they have not. One way to deal with this is by having an agreement and clarity on language. In other words, what does it really mean to call 20 people? At Klemmer & Associates we enroll people for our seminars at various levels. What does it mean to enroll someone? All our employees receive training in the language we use and the definition of certain words. The language of enrollment is not those who fill out a piece of paper. The enrolled are those that have paid in full and specified a date of attendance. A deposit does not count. A form with no money does not count. The specificity of the language assists in telling the truth.

3. **Not telling what is so.** One of the main reasons why people are dishonest is because they don't want to look bad. If you withhold the truth that is also dishonest. I am not suggesting that you begin airing out your dirty laundry to anybody and everybody you meet. You have to use wisdom. But in a situation where you are withholding information with the intent to escape consequences, that too is dishonest, just as dishonest as straightforward open lying.

4. **Pretending not to know.** What are you pretending not to know in your marriage or in your business? It's there, but we subconsciously act as if it is not there. Honesty with your self is as important as honesty with other people. You are not fooling yourself. What you are doing is delaying the process of your own progression by holding yourself back with things that are untrue even though no one else may know. You know you know, so why not just say it? Don't try to fool anyone, because in time you'll be the one that got fooled. There are many average people that never make up a cash flow statement or an asset and liability statement because they don't want to consciously know what it will reveal. They are pretending that because they haven't prepared those statements they don't know. They do know. They are just pretending not to know.

Transparency Versus Honesty

There is a difference between transparency and honesty. Transparency is whereby everything is easily seen. There is always reason for honesty, but not always wisdom in transparency. There are times when transparency is needed and other times when you may want to refrain from being too transparent. If you had an affair 20 years ago, and you no longer live that lifestyle, transparency about the matter would be unnecessary for you to be talking about it.

A compassionate samurai would not do that. It might relieve your guilt, but could very well harm the person you are with. On the other hand, if you were asked whether you had such a situation, honesty would require your answering it truthfully despite it being uncomfortable. The objective of a samurai is "to serve". Transparency should be about helping someone else to overcome in an area that you have overcome also. Transparency has a very definite purpose. Let's look at the definitions:

Transparent—*free from pretense or deceit* : **FRANK** *b* : *easily detected or seen through* : **OBVIOUS** *c* : *readily understood* *d* : *characterized by visibility or accessibility of information especially concerning business practices*

Honesty—*fairness and straightforwardness of conduct* *b* : *adherence to the facts* : **SINCERITY**. **INTEGRITY** *implies trustworthiness and incorruptibility to a degree that one is incapable of being false to a trust, responsibility, or pledge*

Honesty from this definition has to do with integrity and trustworthiness while transparency deals with making yourself visible in such a way that you can be better understood. People at times shy away from both honesty and transparency because they are afraid. With honesty most people always have to weigh out the consequences. People tend to chicken out because they don't want to get yelled at or fired. Look at the example in Enron. The employees there didn't expose the other people that they knew were operating in criminal activities in fear of losing their job.

Have no illusions, there are harmful consequences to being honest. It is why the average person won't be honest. However, what is the cost of not being honest? Usually the cost of not being honest is in loss of intimacy, efficiency and aliveness. The first cost is that it breaks the trust of the other person in you. Once you lie, everything you say begins to be doubted.

Relationships and business are based on trust. Thus we destroy intimacy in relationships and make business inefficient and slow.

The second big cost is that every time you violate your own principles it is like taking a knife and cutting yourself. A piece of you die. It doesn't matter what principle you violate. You become less whole and lack integrity. That is why there are a lot of 40-50 year old walking zombies in this world. They exist, but they are not really alive, and you can see it in them. The average person undervalues transparency, realness, and authenticity.

The people who were involved in the Enron scandal would not be transparent, because transparency would have revealed something about them that they would rather hide. Most people have something about them that they would rather people not know. That's not a problem. You don't have to tell the world everything about you. But there are times when your telling someone else frees you and others. That is the right time to be transparent. People will only follow smarts, competency and image so far. People will follow leaders who are transparent and genuine almost anywhere.

Their transparency gives people a sense of certainty in tough times. The network marketing or multi-level industry is one of the niches we support. It is a phenomenal industry whose reputation has been bruised and tarnished because some people have not been honest. Because honor is one of their dearly held traits, a compassionate samurai would never allow their whole industry reputation to be negatively affected by their behavior or the behavior of anyone else.

The Rich "Big-Time" Liar

The lack of honesty can show up in many ways. Some people buy very expensive cars, fine clothes and luxury houses to make themselves and others feel that they are successful for the purpose of drawing people in with them. That is dishonest or deceitful. People at times buy things they cannot even afford because they know how powerful image is. Image is really what sells people in the short-term scheme of things. Don't tell people that you are making big money if you are not. Let them know that you are in the process of making money.

I'll admit that it doesn't sound really inviting to tell 100 or so fresh prospects that you are saving up for a Lexus, and in about ten months should have enough money to buy it, all from your network marketing business. That doesn't usually sell as quickly. But it may sell, if you try it. That approach may at first surprise a few people; okay it'll shock everybody. But people will have a great deal of respect for your honesty. Honesty breeds trust and trust is essential for a business.

So what if you don't have the Mercedes Benz and the big waterfront estate with a yacht. You have honesty and that goes much further than material things. The traditional samurai used things for its benefit, that's all. They never defined themselves by the things that they used. They only saw those things as tools. When a person defines themselves by things, that process is a never-ending process because things get old. When they get old then they no longer have the same flair that it originally had. And when that defines you, you'll have to always keep up an image just to please people.

The image is not you. The image is really a reflection of very low self-esteem. For the most part, people like this are very seldom transparent or honest. They dread that somebody may know that they are not who they say they are and that they have been living a front for many years. When you lead by image it shows that you are not very interested in going through the process that will afford you the fineries of life the real way. It takes time and commitment to become what you dream of. It may not happen overnight, but that is all right. The process is so valuable that one needs to savor every moment.

Remember that a samurai sword takes 80,000 folds and is heated and beaten repeatedly before it is ready to be presented for use. Maybe before you are presented for show or use you may need to be beaten 80,000 times too. This is only figurative talk. But I hope you are getting the point. Your image is constantly being made. Don't try to become everything overnight. Give it time and be honest in your process. Make small steps toward and celebrate each step and people will honor that quality in you.

What's Your Dirty Little Secret?

Jack Welch in his book <u>Winning</u> calls "lack of candor" the biggest dirty little secret in business. He writes, *"What a huge problem it is. Lack of candor basically blocks smart ideas, fast action, and good people from contributing all the stuff they've got. It's a killer. When you've got candor—and you'll probably never completely get it, mind you—everything just operates faster and better."* (Winning, Pg 25, Harper Collins 2005 copyright)

I agree with Jack. He is perhaps the most successful CEO in American history. If anyone should know about honesty in business and how it affects the overall success of the whole, it's Jack Welch. Honesty helps to make things flow smoother. One of the main things that slow down the progress of organizational development, family progress, personal growth, and even mental expansion is lack of honesty. Be honest with yourself.

What are some areas that you can improve in? Are there areas that you need to grow? Where could you act or take actions far more maturely than you have in the past? Evaluate yourself and give yourself a grade. Be honest. Tell yourself what areas could use a complete overhaul. A samurai does not want yes people around him or her, but desires to surround himself or herself with people that will confront them frankly about areas that they need improvement which will cause them to grow and prosper.

Where could you act or take actions far more
maturely than you have in the past?

Why Be Honest? Because You Care

Why would a person want to be honest in a marriage, in business? What are the benefits? Above we mentioned that honesty makes you more efficient. One of the other primary reasons for your honesty is because you care. If you don't care about anybody or anything then honesty really won't matter much to you. What if your child asks you have you ever used drugs? Should you lie to them as a preventative measure toward them away from drugs?

Absolutely not! Don't tell your kids a lie. Tell the truth. Tell them that you used them, and why you regret it. It's better to be honest and show you care than to have people discover things about you. You ask, "If the question were asked, would I have to reveal everything? What do I have to reveal?" There's no need to get into details. Details only aggravate the situation even more. You tell enough to show you are being honest and in that you are honoring the other person. This honesty develops trust and closeness.

Even though you care, honesty can make things very complicated, in a friendship, marriage, and business. It makes things messy. There are couples married for decades who are not honest with each other about sexual likes and dislikes. Being honest presents a minefield of possible hurt feelings. Average people would rather avoid the discomfort of negotiating that minefield than being honest and dealing with the situation. They trade closeness for comfort. We have been taught that if it's a "white lie" no one is hurt. This is not true. We know it is not the truth.

Many times they can feel it is not true. This is not to say that you can use honesty as an excuse to be cruel. You can find a way to tell the truth and honor the other person.

Two people can get in a relationship and have different expectations. Perhaps one sees this as a permanent relationship. Perhaps the other person is just going along for the ride and it is simply a relationship of convenience. The average person is afraid of losing what they have and either avoids the conversation or uses vague language. Perhaps they are receiving benefits like gifts, dinners, and nights out on the town.

It's not honest to just continue on without dealing with the situation. You may want to say, "Let's slow things down. We are going too fast in this relationship." If you say let's slow down, it may jeopardize your gift flow. That really doesn't matter. Complications will come either now or later. A compassionate samurai will honor the other person and the principle of honesty by declaring where they are. A whole society can collectively be dishonest. In the United States for many years, many Americans turned a blind eye to the damages of segregation.

Currently many people are turning a blind eye to the effects of environmental damage or the deterioration of our schools. Some people who are very overweight or are in poor health are not being honest with themselves. They are dishonest in the sense that they convince themselves that they can continue on eating anything, anytime, anywhere and that they'll be fine.

In time, that'll catch up with you and kill you. The sooner you deal with it the better your chances of survival. That goes for all areas of life. Prevention is always the best method for dealing with things. Compassionate samurai deal with things before they start and before they get out of hand. But, you will only use preventative measures when you sincerely and whole-heartedly care about yourself and the loved ones who care about you.

Honesty—The Two-Edged Sword

Most people are generally not prepared for the repercussions of honesty. That is why they tend to shy away from it. Being honest is like paying cash instead of using a credit card. You pay the little prices up front and suffer some discomfort with cash. With a credit card you live in an illusion of comfort until one day the piper needs to be paid and you suffer depression.

Honesty is much like a two-edge sword. It can cut, but at the same time it's other side can cause mending. That's the power of the sword. Often things have to be cut before things can start to heal. That's not always comfortable but it's effective. So there are benefits to honesty that one will receive when they choose this compassionate samurai's path.

Benefits of honesty

1. Increases intimacy—if I care about a relationship being a deep meaningful relationship, it will only come through honesty. Intimacy means **In-to-me- I see**. If I want intimacy, honesty is a must.

2. It brings more people and their creativity into the process. When I was honest with what I was working within myself, other people started to become more honest too. In the work place, if I am looking for greater buy in or commitment from the people, I will be honest. They'll be more committed than complain.

84

3. It speeds things up. It takes the clutter out of things. It saves time and makes things more efficient.

Using Diplomacy

Here's a final word. Don't use the principle of honesty to justify being obnoxious and make people feel less than human. Use tact. It's not beneficial to berate people just because you notice an area that they may need improvement. Did you even ask their permission to give them feedback? In our company, I have watched conversations where one person asks, "Can I give you some feedback?" The other person has responded, "No. I have other things on my mind and I won't hear it. Please give it to me tomorrow." What a great honest conversation!

If someone agrees to receive feedback, there is always a way to say what you need to say to someone without coming off as rude and impolite. Furthermore, be aware that your criticism of others frequently says more about the one communicating than it does the receiver of the feedback. *You can only criticize in others that which reflects your own experience. You can only identify in others the things that are easily detected in you.* The only difference between them and you is that theirs is noticeable and your issue is concealed.

You can only criticize in others that which reflects your own experience.
You can only identify in others the things that are easily detected in you.

Qualify your intentions before dealing with a person concerning a matter. What is your intent in being honest? Be honest about your intentions. Is your intention really to help the other person or is it to make them feel bad? If your intention is the latter, then keep your suggestions to yourself regardless of whether they are honest or not. There is always a certain way to approach a matter. If you really want to help, know that the way you approach a matter will determine the outcome. What you may have intended for good can be obscured and turn out not so good because you went about it the wrong way.

Use your mind and better judgment before entering a situation that involves your honesty toward someone else. In fact, the best honesty and the best observations are usually toward oneself. Master that first before trying those skills out on other people. Many people have been taught how to say "the right" things in various situations. But just saying the right things cannot cover up the real you. Whatever your real desire is, will always be revealed. So, it's a whole lot better to deal honestly up front. If you don't, in time your true desires and motives are going to be exposed. There really aren't any secrets.

When that happens you look bad, and the person whom you told what they wanted to hear has pretty much lost all faith in your word. Perhaps a building contractor gives a client what they want to hear. They say, "The work will be totally finished in a month." When the job winds up taking two months to complete the client is angry, the contractor is scarred and frustrated, knowing that he may be sued for breeching the contract. He told the customer what he wanted to hear, yet did not have true intentions on following through on his word. This happens all of the time. Say what you'll do.

Do what you say. The average person will say something like "I'll try and...". It is the illusion of commitment. *Trying is lying.* Having an exit door in place, just in case something does not go as expected, is avoiding the truth. You can't get into something expecting it to go sour. If you do that, it will go sour.

Many people get married with the intention of escaping if something goes wrong. They commit to each other with vows (giving each other what they want to hear, and of course the attendees too) with less than honest intentions.

The point is that no matter what you say, everybody will really know where your heart was and is in time. The cure is to just be honest. Contractors, let your client know up front that you are working on a big job three towns over, and that you took their job to keep revenue flowing so you can meet payroll. Let them know that it may take longer than normal, perhaps two or three months to complete the job, but you'll throw in some extras for their patience. Your honesty may lose some customers, but it will also attract many others.

And before you say I do, sit down and have an honest talk about all of the things that might cause you to take flight in your marriage early on. "If this happens I'm not going to stick around. I'm gone!" Okay that's pretty blunt, but at least it's honest. Your spouse may not want to hear that, but will appreciate it in the long run. But after all of the talk your truth is the only thing that people see. The traditional samurai did not have many words at all. They were relatively quiet people. It's not that they could not talk; they understood the power of words and did not want to use them flippantly. The samurai realized that silence would cause them to take action, at times quicker than words.

> *"I hope I shall possess firmness and virtue enough to maintain what I consider the most enviable of all titles, the character of an honest man."*
>
> —George Washington

Compassionate samurai hold principles above personal benefit.

Average people do whatever is best for themselves.

"Integrity is the essence of everything successful."
—Unknown.

Chapter Six

Honor

To honor is to hold in high esteem and respect. Every major religion has a tenet to hold parents in high esteem. Yet, in our society dishonor runs rampant and can be easily found. People really don't understand the importance of honoring others even at a very base level. Children dishonor their parents. Some children lie to their parents, others swear at and perform acts of open rebelliousness in front of them. Sports players are spitting at each other and hitting referees. Steroid use by athletes is known and officials turn a blind eye with only token policies.

Taunting became so commonplace and frequent it had to be specified as a penalty. Politicians think nothing of throwing "dirt" at an opponent. It's just part of the game. Nobody expects them to tell the truth. Lawyers are one of the least thought of professions because they are known for doing whatever it takes regardless of principles. There is the old adage "there is honor among thieves." Kids are joining gangs for honor because they can't find it any other places. A couple years ago, a member of the Dixie Chicks country-singing group, made some derogatory remarks about our president.

Tens of thousands of Americans burned and trashed their CD's in response. What was most amazing is that in the interviews that ensued, the lead singer couldn't understand that reaction. She thought people weren't respecting the right of free speech. The reality was, very few people had an issue with their anti-war viewpoint. Half the country disagrees with the president. The only thing they reacted to was her name calling and trashing of the president. Dishonor always carries a very high price to pay. It costs the one doing the dishonor. It costs the person it was done to and it costs everyone affiliated with the one doing the dishonoring behavior.

The price that one may pay for dishonor is not always immediately recognized. Just because it is not recognized does not mean that it is not paid. Society tends to hide the affects and consequences of dishonor. They make it seem as though if you do not show honor that you will get away with it. The truth is that you never "get away with" not showing honor. It'll catch up to you sooner or later. A person who understands honor understands that in honoring the person you are dealing with, you are essentially honoring yourself, honoring your family, honoring your work group or any other affiliation you have, even the samurai name. The traditional samurai even honored their enemies.

Honoring Whoever You Interact With

I asked a high level executive friend named Tim Redmond, to come in for a couple of days, observe me, and let me know what adjustments I needed to make to become and lead a $100 million dollar a year company. Among his feedback was a comment that floored me. He said, on the one hand, I had a vision that inspired him, empowered people, saw the best in them, and paid them more than he would. On the other hand, he said that I was condescending toward my employees. I was shocked.

Perhaps I was in gross denial because I never saw myself as being this way toward anyone, especially my employees. I asked for him to explain in further detail. He asked me to recall the conversations I had throughout the day with people in our office. I reflected. He then said I didn't have any conversations I basically had monologues. I would be telling people what to do, not asking their opinion. Not giving people a chance to offer their viewpoint on what needed to be done, is simply condescending. It was not honoring their value as a Klemmer & Associates teammate.

Since then I have been working on starting off every conversation with a question. That's an honoring behavior. It basically says I value your input. Asking the consultant, Tim Redmond, to give me feedback was an honoring behavior to him and myself. I have now told my employees they have my permission to tell me when I forget to start off a conversation with a question. That's another honoring behavior. You can be honest without having a condescending or belittling attitude toward people. But the first way to do this is by hearing them out.

When a compassionate samurai communicates with others,
their highest goal is to first be a listener.

As simple as this lesson may sound, it is really a very big problem for a lot of people, especially controllers and high achievers. At times, high achievers feel as if they have earned the right not to listen to anyone else since they have already "arrived in life." Nothing could be further from the truth. The higher you go up in life the more input you are going to regularly need to stay there. You may have heard the true phrase, "the bigger they are the harder they fall."

I'd much rather listen to others advice and instruction and preserve the fruits of my labor than to lose it all through my arrogance and pride.

When a compassionate samurai communicates with others, their highest goal is to first be a listener. Intent listening shows that you honor the person with whom you are communicating. And of course you always learn far more through listening than you will ever learn through just talking. Perhaps it is why God gave us two ears and only one mouth. Keeping your agreements with others, even when they appear to be small, is a mark of honor. Showing up on time whether it is for meetings or coming home from work is an honoring behavior.

Average people today think nothing of being late and it communicates what I have to do is more important than what you have to do. I have seen executives repeatedly keep a hundred people waiting. It is dishonoring. Simply talking well of other people is honoring. Some people don't ever give credit for anything to other people. That is dishonoring. Think about your boss or up-line in your business. When was the last time you edified and built them up to someone else? Perhaps you are thinking there is nothing to edify.

There is always something good to find in someone else, whether it is his or her sincerity, determination, or fun spirit. Perhaps you are thinking they don't deserve it. That is all the more reason to edify and honor them. Sow into them without them even knowing. It will make you look good. What can you do to honor your children? What do you do? Most importantly, what will you do? Do you give them one-on-one time? Do you ask their opinion? Are they encouraged to participate in conversations with adults? Do you hold them capable of solving problems or are you always solving their problems for them?

One of the people I frequently talk about is my mentor, Tom. I tell people how my life is different because of him. I wouldn't be a best selling author, I wouldn't have raised millions of dollars for causes I believe in, I wouldn't be married, I wouldn't be a Christian, and on and on if it wasn't for him. It has been 24 years since he was killed. It is part of what I do to honor him. Like most people, he had his faults, some of which were pretty severe. I never mention those. I talk about my own faults instead. There is no way I can ever repay him, but this is the right thing to do.

That is what a compassionate samurai does. How many times have you heard someone complain about his or her organization? A compassionate samurai never does that. A compassionate samurai will go to the person or to management and register a complaint. That actually honors them. Doing that says I care enough about you and this organization to go to someone who can do something about the situation. They never complain to people who can't do anything about the situation. Average people complain to whoever will listen.

How can you honor the organization you work for? Not only can you speak well of the organization, you can look out for it. Abusing an expense account dishonors the company that is paying your check and the co-workers you work with. Leaving a communal kitchen at work a mess dishonors both the company and your co-workers. Average people do what's best for themselves regardless of the impact on others. Average people will make a sale whether it is good for the other person or not. Average people increase their income and lifestyle even if it pollutes the environment.

Compassionate samurai would not dishonor future generations. How could you honor service people you interact with throughout your day? This could be a waiter, a retail sales clerk, a janitor at the office, or a bank teller. Do you know their name and use it? People love when you use their name as the customer. People even expect that as part of good service. The average person does not return the honoring behavior, although it is so easy and simple to do. Do you take people that serve you for granted or do you ask a question or two that honors them and contributes to their day? What kind of a tip do you leave them?

What tone of voice do you use when you are at the airport and there has been a delay? A compassionate samurai is always looking to serve and to honor other human beings. You may have heard about the practice of tithing and giving the first 10% of your earnings to God or where you get your spiritual nourishment. Tithing is an honoring practice. For those that do it, they are honoring God by giving the first fruits. It is an acknowledgement that God is the source of all things, instead of relying solely on our own intellect, or skills. This honors God.

A compassionate samurai is always looking to serve
and to honor other human beings.

Honoring Yourself

When you look at honor, honor is really about respect. When the word respect is mentioned, it is commonly used as it relates to respecting others. You've heard the phrases, "Respect your elders. Honor your mother and your father. Give honor to whom honor is due." All of those phrases ring a familiar tone in your hearing. But how about this phrase, "Honor yourself." Does that feel right to you? If it does not, it is only because you've not heard the phrase enough times for it to form a habit in your mind and actions.

You may be surprised just how many people really don't have a healthy respect for themselves. When people do not have a healthy respect for themselves it always shows. You can't hide it. One way to determine if people have a healthy respect for themselves is by watching how that person keeps their own word to themselves. If you cannot commit to do for you what you say you are going to do, then you really don't honor yourself. There are people who give to others, but never give to themselves. That is not honoring.

There are people who make time for spouses, time for children, time for work, time for church, time for friends, but who feel guilty about taking time for themselves. That is not honoring you. You deserve to treat yourself well. A compassionate samurai will do things for themselves, whether it is a massage, spend time in the hot tub, or read. That is not selfish unless it is carried to the extreme of not having time for others. If you don't take care of yourself, you will eventually be a martyr and not be any good for anyone else. Service is a bottomless pit. You always want to contribute, but do not fall into the trap of thinking you can finish or complete your duty.

Do you exercise and eat right? That is a self-honoring practice. What do you say to yourself when you make a mistake? Do you honor yourself with saying it was a good effort and look for the lesson learned? Do you dishonor yourself by berating yourself and putting yourself down with comments like, "that was the stupidest thing ever?" The samurai honored himself very highly. That is the main reason why he felt so compelled to honor other people that he came into contact with, even his enemies. How he treated himself was an indication of his overall healthy image. It is that kind of image that others see in you, and that image you can give to others. How you treat your-self is a direct reflection of how you will treat others in life.

The Power of Your Mentor

Vulnerability is more attractive than invincibility. Being trained in the army I was taught the opposite concept. I make it a point to talk about my mentor often to show honor. Some people feel weird talking about other people because they have an issue with honor, because they really don't honor themselves. Others operate from scarcity and are afraid to bring people on stage or give recognition. Everybody acts like they invented this or that, when in all reality very few people originate. We improve on what others have already popularized long before our time. King Solomon was quite right when he said that there is nothing new under the sun.

Every time I mention my mentor's name, Tom Whilhite, I actually honor myself and increase the value of my personal worth. People trust me more when I unashamedly identify with another man, letting people know without reservation that he is responsible in a large part for the success that I enjoy today. One thing that most achievers have in common is that they all can say that they have a mentor whom they credit their knowledge and success with. An average person sees life so differently than compassionate samurai. Compassionate samurai see life through the eyes of interdependence not independence as average people do.

There really is no such thing as independence. It's a misnomer. Everybody is connected whether we want to acknowledge that truth or not. It is when we realize how powerful our connectedness is that we realize and actualize our collective worth. Without someone to follow I am lost. People that are lost cannot make meaningful contributions to the universe. It is important to hook up with a mentor, someone that can lead you to where you belong: someone that has been there already.

Dishonor Makes You Small

Dishonor diminishes a person's value. Some years ago, Mike Tyson during a championship fight bit Evander Holyfield during his match. It shocked the entire sports world that he would do such an animalistic thing. When he did this, he was disqualified, fined, and reprimanded by the boxing association. He dishonored himself and fans dropped him like a hot potato. The ramification was not only toward Mike Tyson for his actions but the whole boxing profession. The whole industry began to look like a joke. Mike Tyson's family was embarrassed.

The traditional samurai would kill themselves by <u>seppuku</u> rather than embarrass their family or group. Seppuku was an incredible act of courage where they stabbed themselves in the stomach and made seven sideways strokes. Their body died but their reputation lived on. Mike Tyson was a great fighter, the champion of the world. But in one moments time he went from looking big and strong to appearing weak and small before all of the people that were viewing him all around the world. His dishonor made him look small.

There are people that do things that dishonor their family name, particularly in families that have long-standing traditions of wealth and contribution. If you belong to a wealthy and respectable bloodline, you have to be careful who you connect with, who you date, and who you even socialize with. You can't hang out with criminals when you have a name to uphold. In one sense my children have had it tough in that since I founded Klemmer & Associates Leadership Seminars; they could not act like normal kids sometimes.

They realized it could affect business and the reputation I have spent years building. In another sense it was good. I think all people can look at themselves as royalty with a name to uphold. In some families it may not be obvious, but it is there nonetheless. At WestPoint, the United States Military Academy, we learned the values of Duty—Honor—Country. These are the core values of the motto. It is the code of a compassionate samurai. Did you do your duty? It doesn't matter whether you liked it or not. Duty comes first.

You honored your country and military unity as well as yourself by doing your duty. An average person might consider letting him or herself down, but you could not let your unit or country down. They had the honor code, which said you couldn't lie, cheat, or steal or tolerate anyone who did. Honor required you to turn the cadets in that violated any of those codes if you knew about it. The civilian world called this ratting someone out. We believed that this was upholding the overall reputation of all our fellow cadets.

You cared so much about that reputation you would turn your best friend in. That is the level of commitment to principles of a compassionate samurai. This was a value that took most of the cadets time to get into their head. You could violate a regulation like drinking alcohol on campus. If caught that carried a certain punishment like walking the area and confinement to quarters for a while. If you lied about the fact that you drank, then that violated the honor code and you were expelled. No lie was too small to exempt you from expulsion. It only took one time.

If you were asked if you shined your shoes and you said yes when you hadn't, you were expelled. Outsiders sometimes thought this was too severe, but cadets rarely did. It established an unbelievable context to live our lives by. In the beginning many of the cadets followed out of fear of being expelled. Over time they moved from compliance to the code to a true commitment to the code. A compassionate samurai has the highest of standards and measures himself or herself by that standard, not what the world standard is.

A Compassionate Samurai's Actions Affects Everybody

It's one thing to dishonor yourself, but you can never do just that. Your actions reflect on all your affiliations such as your work group, whatever faith you belong to, your country, and all other compassionate samurai. A samurai's actions are never his or her own. They collectively share their actions with everyone else. When a samurai dies you have to honor them by bowing before them, even if they are on the enemy's side. If they do not properly honor their opponents they will die as punishment for not honoring their opponent.

In modern vernacular we may call this idea team loyalty and support. Life is really about being on a very HUGE team. Our facilitators all sign an ethics code. If they have sex with a student or use illegal drugs they will be let go. There are seminar companies and individual speakers who use their platform and position of authority to take sexual advantages. Life on the road away from home has its temptations. Such acts would not only dishonor them, it would dishonor all of Klemmer & Associates Leadership Seminars as well as their families.

You can't win in life in the most real sense until everybody wins.

For most of our team the threat of being let go creates compliance to the code, but the desire not to reflect poorly and let down their coworkers who have done incredible things for them are what creates commitment. It is this realization and experience of duty to the team that upholds their honor. You can't win in life in the most real sense until everybody wins. Unfortunately, we have come so far away from this concept of win-win, that we have lost the sense of living to help others live and in the process gain a profound sense of life.

Average people never care about their actions or who it affects. They just live each day for their own individual pleasure not thinking twice about the trail of negative seeds they are sowing. Average people don't think about others. They think only of themselves, because they are selfish. Compassionate samurais live their life for the value, benefit and reputation of others, of their team as a whole.

Compassionate samurai hold principles above personal benefit.
Average people do whatever is best for themselves

Grad Story

In 2003 Bill Kelly took our seminars. He is a real estate broker who at his peak prior to that year had made $200,000 a year and had worked himself ragged to do it. I purchased a four-plex residential building in Santa Rosa, CA from him and complimented him on what appeared to be significant weight loss. He had lost 53 pounds and kept it off for a year. I asked him how he had lost the weight. He teased me replying, <u>If How To's Were</u>

<u>Enough, We Would All Be Skinny Rich and Happy,</u> silly (The title of my first best selling book). He then explained that in our Samurai Camp he had established the habit of honor.

With respecting himself he began to honor his body. Once he honored himself he started working out regularly on the treadmill. He realized that certain foods were hindering his overall healthiness and causing the weight to stay on him. With that he began to choose foods that would help his overall health, not encumber it. He no longer reached for potato chips, sodas, and candy as his quick fix but rather began making sensible choices like vegetables, fruits, and water. He viewed eating the bad foods as lacking honor for his body.

Instead of viewing working out as drudgery, he looked at working out as honoring his body. Needless to say, Bill lost the weight and has maintained a healthy figure. He did not do it from high impact dieting, or overworking himself out at the gym, but through choosing to look at his physical body as a vessel of honor, only worthy of the best treatment and the highest quality select foods. It's not that how to's are bad. It's that how to's by themselves are insufficient.

People know how to lose weight. Eat less and work out more. Our behavior however is driven by beliefs in our heart. Bill's income that year skyrocketed to over $600,000. People like to be around those who honor themselves. It has attracted clients. It has affected the type and quality of client he has attracted. The best news of all is that he has done it by working less and increasing the quality of his marriage and lifestyle. It is an honor approach.

"Integrity is the essence of everything successful." —*Unknown*

A compassionate samurai has the capacity to trust others and themselves with their life and have the wisdom to know when to do so.

Average people are either unwilling to trust others to be as trustworthy as they are or trust blindly without doing due diligence.

Chapter Seven

Trust

"You may be deceived if you trust too much, but you will live in torment if you do not trust enough." —Dr. Frank Crane.

One of the most overused and under appreciated phrases is "I Love You." These words have so much power, yet when put to the test to prove one's love for another, so many fail the test. The main reason for this is that those words are not always well thought through before saying them. For many, those words are used as a tool to gain access to certain areas in life. Men have used that phrase many times over to sweep the woman of his dreams off her feet. After he got from her what he wanted, perhaps he took her for granted or even started treating her like dirt. The relationship was lost.

That of course is not always the case. But when it does happen, why does it happen? Trust was broken. The words I love you have the power to gain access but do not have the power to keep you at the point of your desire once you arrive there. Trust can maintain a relationship through many difficult challenges. That is true in business or personal relationships. For the most part the words "I love you," have become weakened since they are used so often without much conviction behind them. That's quite unfortunate because this phrase really does carry a power packed punch when used properly and thoughtfully.

Compassionate samurai have the capacity to trust others and themselves with their life and have the wisdom to know when to do so.

The phrase, "I Trust You," can carry equal power and punch, if not more when used appropriately. These are three very powerful words. However there are so many people that are scared to death to use the phrase, and are unable to trust themselves or others to any large capacity. Some don't even see the benefits to trusting. Compassionate samurai have the capacity to trust others and themselves with their life and have the wisdom to know when to do so. If you want to be a compassionate samurai and lead an extraordinary life than you MUST know how to trust.

In today's world many of us were brought up not to trust. I was taught very young that it was a dog-eat-dog world and that if you don't look out for yourself, no one else will. It is true in my experience that much of the world operates from non-trust. Does that mean you have to? No. Do you want to be ordinary or extra-ordinary? To be and produce "extra-ordinary" you must be able to trust. Persons that have been the victims of seriously abused trust may find it hard to trust, but they can. Love can overlook many imperfections. Trust does not. Trust demands perfection. Unlike love, trust must be earned.

What is trust? Trust is relying on the character, ability, and word of a person. People sometimes will say, "I trust you." But what does that mean? If I say I trust you to one of my children that may mean I trust them to come home by curfew. I trust them to not do illegal drugs. Yet I do not trust them to make the financial decisions for my company. Trust is item specific. So to simply say I trust you is an inaccurate and misleading statement.

Why trust?

Unless you see the benefits of trusting you may be tempted to slide through life without trusting. There are five benefits that motivate a compassionate samurai to trust.

- It is the only way to access the synergistic power of teamwork.

- It builds relationship and intimacy.

- It releases time freedom and efficiency.

- It's the primary tool for making a difference and being of service.

- You receive an exhilarating feeling.

First let's deal with the synergistic power of teamwork. Synergy is the idea that the whole is greater than the sum of the individual parts. $1 + 1 = 3$. Suppose you can only lift 50 pounds with your left arm and only 50 pounds with your right arm. Normal math would indicate you could only lift 100 pounds using both arms. In reality you end up lifting about 140 pounds. Where does that extra 40 pounds come from? It is a scientific phenomenon known as synergy.

In the financial arena if three or four people pool their resources whether it is simply their money, time, or specific investment knowledge, they can get much higher rates of return. With only $10,000 to invest you have certain opportunities. With $100,000 to invest many more opportunities are open to you. With $1,000,000 to invest you have even more. But to pool your resources requires that you trust each other. Many people don't want to trust others in that situation thinking that they will run off with their money.

"I wouldn't want to work hard looking for an investment if they aren't." No one wants to be taken advantage of. But if I don't trust I cannot have team, and synergy. Then I am condemned to being ordinary. I'll be a big fish but only in a little pond. Secondly, without trust, even if you made it to your desired destination, you would be alone and lonely. You will be at your arrival point with no one to share your wins with. In the movie "The Godfather," Al Pacino, the Godfather gets to the top by trusting certain people.

He employed the synergistic power of team. As the movie and series progressed however, trust was eroded and eventually he was all by himself. Certain people in business will step on people to get ahead or simply not share recognition with others. Trust is broken. When that happens not only are they alone, but also no one is eager to help them. Their power is reduced. This relates to the third benefit of time freedom and efficiency. When a person doesn't trust they are unable to delegate. Yes they can do a great job themselves, but now they must do everything.

Their ability is limited by the hours in the day. By trusting they can unleash the wondrous power of leverage and get work done even when they are not working. Opportunities can be seized that would have been missed. Huge burdens can be lifted from your shoulders. I love fund raising for great causes. If I simply gave my money I could only give so much. When I ask others to trust me and to trust themselves that they are capable of replacing what they give then we create even more money through exponential increase from what I could give alone. It inspires more people to get the job done. We do more together than if we acted alone.

In a work environment where trust is lacking, information flow slows to a crawl. It becomes inefficient. In the average workplace honest feedback is a rare thing? Why? Trust has been broken. Perhaps someone got vulnerable and trusted someone with sensitive information and it was used against him or her.

Perhaps the feedback was given not with the intent of uplifting the person, but to make them feel bad about a mistake. Trying to make decisions with less information will cause one to not only make poorer decisions, but also have a hesitancy to even make decisions, since they know they lack pertinent information.

The fourth benefit is that it is the primary tool of making a difference or contributing. When you trust someone you empower him or her. They play at a higher level trying to live up to the trust you have placed in them. In our process of training facilitators there is a point where the trainer of the trainers starts leaving the room for longer and longer periods of time. Students will always comment how the facilitator trainee 'magically' transforms and becomes almost another person as they are living up to the trust placed in them. If you want to make a difference you must learn to empower others by trusting them.

The fifth benefit is that trusting another human being or yourself produces an exhilarating feeling. It's a high. It's a rush. There's nothing wrong with that. A compassionate samurai deserves to feel great. Think about a time in your life where you trusted someone to do something and they came through. Perhaps it was the first day you let one of your children drive your car without you in it. Maybe it was when you first let your child walk or ride their bike to school on their own. It could have been the time that you bought your first house and trusted yourself enough to pay off the mortgage. Do you remember how they felt? Do you remember how you felt? You were on a high.

So with all these benefits why aren't more people trusting? Trust carries its risks. You can be hurt more and quicker when you trust. You lose control when you trust. If I trust you to do a job, now you are making many decisions, not me. There are simply different benefits and prices to trusting and not trusting. It's all a matter of what you want to deal with. A compassionate samurai takes the maximum gain strategy of trusting whenever possible versus the average person plays not to lose by not trusting.

The Risk Reward Ratio

Some people find themselves as the perpetual victim of abusiveness. I am sure you have seen people who have had their trust of another person violated and where they continually give people their trust and their heart without putting them through any kind of screening process. Perhaps you have seen people invest large amounts of money simply because they find out a celebrity has invested in the same project. They did not do any investigating or due diligence. That is not trust. That's being irresponsible. Trust must be earned. It is built by continually risking increasing amounts of money, time, authority, your heart, or any other resource.

The compassionate samurai is trusting and receives trust also, but does not willingly go into danger zones expecting to be disappointed. That's not intelligent at all. The samurai is always ready to give their trust to another person even a stranger. They will not hold innocent newcomers accountable for breeching trust if they were not the ones that breeched their trust. Yet at the same time, they don't just go around trusting people that have a proven track record of failure in the trust area.

The first type of individual is the person that tends to be a glutton for unnecessary pain trusting anybody and everybody without any sense of knowledge or inner conviction that the person is capable of being worthy of your trust. Years ago I was recommended to a financial investment person named Josh Murakami. A successful financial friend had some money invested with Josh. I did not simply invest with Josh because my friend did. Yet I see many people invest tens of thousands of dollars, simply based on a recommendation. A compassionate samurai would not do that.

I performed some due diligence. What were his credentials? How much money did he manage and for how long with what rates of return? I did not simply take Josh's word for results; I talked with current and previous investors. Surely you have received advertisements from investment newsletters where they make incredible claims of always predicting the stock market. Just because they make a prediction you don't have to believe them. You check them out. After my checking out process, I decided to invest some money with Josh. Did I invest all my investment capital? No.

I invested $25,000, an amount at that time I could afford to lose. It wouldn't have affected my lifestyle at all. I wouldn't be happy losing the money, but it wouldn't be that big a deal. So I tested his performance for a year. He returned 50% on the money and gave monthly reports on all the trades. So then I put more money in. He returned 50% again. The third year was about a 15% gain. He has earned more trust by managing the money and giving returns. In our business, certain employees do not have any authority to spend money without it being first approved.

Another level of employee can make a $500 purchase. They have shown how they think and what kind of decisions they make and that's why we promoted them. They earned our trust to spend at that level without checking. A management team member could make a $5000 decision without checking. They have earned that authority. If they made several poor decisions they would lose our trust and consequently lose that authority.

The same thinking around trust applies in relationships. Some people will make a huge commitment like marriage and not do any do diligence. That is not trust. That is not responsible. Due diligence is asking tough value questions before you get married. Find out about their past. Get to know their parents. My wife, Roma, and I have been married 22 years as I am writing this. For all that time I have been on the road traveling at least half the time doing seminars. Because of her due diligence with me she trusted me that I would not have an affair. It was hard, but she made that choice.

All that traveling that I do certainly provides the opportunities, but a compassionate samurai would never have an affair because it would violate the principle of honor. It would dishonor my family name, my wife, our company's reputation, and the very name of a samurai. I have never had an affair. The years of making the right choices have earned her trust even further where she doesn't even give it a thought.

There is also the question of trusting ourselves. What do we trust ourselves to be able to do and not to do? I would never bring a woman to my hotel room for a meeting of any kind without at least a couple gentlemen also being present. Not only would it be a bad perception problem even if nothing happened, but I have everything to lose if I failed in a moment of loneliness and temptation for only a minimal amount of pleasure.

In business there is a principle called the risk reward ratio. It simply means that there is no significance without knowing both. If I told you to put ten thousand dollars up and you had a 90 percent chance of losing would you do it? You can't make that decision. It means nothing. If I tell you that you have a 90 percent chance of losing and the return if you win is $1,000,000 now you have a ratio and a significant number. Now you can make a decision. You could have a 99 percent chance of winning but your reward is only a dollar and again now you have that ratio.

A compassionate samurai considers this in the arena of trust. They have the capacity to trust totally, but are wise about when and where they place that trust. Do you trust yourself to pick the right person to be in relationship with? Do you trust yourself that if an employee makes a mistake you can recover it? Do you trust yourself to make the right decision? Do you trust God will really provide for you? You must build up and earn trust in yourself just like you do in others. When you fail to trust others, it is not always other people that have the problem or may appear to be suspicious.

The samurai's approach to that is simply to learn the lesson
from what happened and move on.

Usually your lack of being able to trust others identifies a much greater problem within you. Often your inability to trust others means that you are not trustworthy. The other extreme is equally as unfruitful, and that is the person who because another person violated them chooses to close the door to anybody from ever entering in their life. Although, I realize that this is a self-protection mechanism, it doesn't work. It doesn't make valid and reasonable sense. Every samurai knows what it feels like to have been hurt and double-crossed in a situation whether that situation was a business deal, a relationship, or even in a close friendship. The samurai's approach to that is simply to learn the lesson from what happened and move on.

Gone In A Seconds Time.

A true samurai knows very well that they will need the interdependent support of a team in order to accomplish their life's purpose and mission. If they become paranoid because of a negative situation that arose they will never fulfill their goals in life. Early in Klemmer & Associates history I trained someone to be a facilitator. They were a very good facilitator. Then I made them a partner sharing equity in revenue generated. He had made some poor private financial decisions and became financially challenged.

Then he got greedy and tried to steal the business. He did not succeed. I thought that we'd established a good working relationship and friendship over many years. But in the moment of his greed and ill-thought actions, all of the trust that I had for him and in him was suddenly gone. I didn't lose trust in him because I thought that he was perfect and could do no wrong, but rather because I did not believe that he would breech our trust over money. I'm not sure that there is a legitimate reason to breech trust at all, but a compassionate samurai would never breech trust over money.

To the compassionate samurai money is a means of exchange. It is an illusion to which we give a value. From one point of view, it is not real. It is only as real as we make it out to be. Money is easily replaceable, not rare. It does not have an intrinsic value. It is actually paper notes that can be easily destroyed by fire, water, or even blown away by the wind. So to lose a relationship over money is a reversal of values to a compassionate samurai and not something they would ever do. He has even asked to work for us again, but it won't happen. Why? Risk reward ratio.

There is really little to gain by having him come back, since I can train other great facilitators. There is much to lose though, in time, energy, heartache, finances etc. I forgave the man, and I can honestly say that I love him and wish him well. I just don't trust him any longer with our company's future. However, can a compassionate samurai trust someone else to be a partner? Absolutely, but an average person would not. In fact, several years ago we trusted two long-term Klemmer and Associates team members, Patrick Dean and Steve Hinton to become partners.

It was necessary to create the synergistic power and leverage. It has paid off handsomely for everyone and we have touched many more lives than if I had run the show by myself. Trust can be viewed much like the construction of a skyscraper. It may take several months to draw up the blueprints for the building. Then to assemble the right crews to do the work could take months. The building itself could take years to build from start to finish. Yet the right force against the building can take it down in less than an hour. Breech of trust can have such an incredibly strong impact against a relationship, that it can quickly destroy that relationship.

A compassionate samurai understands how to gain, manage, and grow trust. Perhaps you have heard people say things like "I don't trust anybody anymore." When people say things like this, it's easy to identify that they've been badly hurt by someone's broken trust. In reality when people say this they aren't really being honest. No matter how much you want to bar yourself from ever trusting anyone again, it's not that easy to accomplish. As long as you are alive you really have to trust people over and again. If you believe that you don't trust anyone, then why are you reading this book?

You would have to trust the author and somehow believe that I may have something of value to say to you. You trusted whomever you gave money to purchase this book. Did they give you back the appropriate change or did they rob you? It took trust to expect that they'd give you back your proper change. Did you purchase this book with a check? If you did, did you make sure that the person whom you gave the check to did not take down your bank's routing number and account number?

A compassionate samurai does not try to escape trusting others,

but rather looks for opportunities to extend their trust to others.

It is very possible that they may be able to tap into your account and illegally withdraw funds from your account. If you gave them a credit card, the person may charge your card to the max. Gracious! I could go on and on, but

I'm sure that you are getting the point. In the most basic sense we are almost coerced each day into trusting others, from catching a subway or train, or even something as simple as trusting a fellow driver to stay on their side of the road.

You can't escape giving others your trust. A compassionate samurai does not try to escape trusting others, but rather looks for opportunities to extend their trust to others. The samurai knows that their very life is many times totally at the mercy of someone whom they've trusted. To withdraw trust is to withdraw life. And to withdraw life prematurely is aborting your mission, something that a samurai never does.

Inspect What You Expect

Here is a gross misconception. People think that if you check on them that you don't trust them. That's untrue. Just because you inspect doesn't mean that you don't trust. It really means that you are being a good steward over your time, your investments, and over people whom you've been entrusted to care for. You may have seen this with children and their parents. The parent will tell the child to do a particular chore, and when the parents inspect the child's performance, the child screams out, "You don't trust me." It's not that the parent doesn't trust the child; the parent has a responsibility to inspect what they've ordered.

The inspection actually increases trust when the job has been done as requested. It provides feedback from which to make course corrections and keep you on course. There is an old business adage that you must inspect what you expect. Scuba divers always go with a partner. They check each other's tanks. It is not that they think their partner is incompetent and don't trust them. It is because of the risk ratio formula. So much is at stake—a human life. The odds are we can make a little mistake that costs a huge amount so it doesn't matter if the odds are only one in a thousand.

Even in a marriage this concept still holds true, although there must be some fine tuning depending on the marriage and the people involved. If a husband or wife, continually promises to be home at a certain time, yet always has an excuse when they don't show up on time, it will break the other person's trust. They might not trust you to show up on time as a minimum. It can bleed into other areas where they wonder if I can't trust them with time, what else can I not trust them for? This is why a compassionate samurai would never lie, cheat or steal.

When trust is broken in your word, nothing else can be trusted. Honesty is the very foundation of trust. It has been said that during the cold war President Reagan and President Gorbachev had a meeting where President Reagan said to Mr. Gorbachev, "Look. The truth is I don't trust you. You don't trust me. Given that, where do we go from here?" It was from that very honesty that the whole Berlin wall came down.

Some people take the idea of inspecting what you expect to an extreme and check everything all the time. That is inefficient and not trusting. They value control more than increased production. Remember risk reward: what is at stake and what have they proven? The more that a person has proven and the less that is at stake the less you should be checking.

The compassionate samurai does not take the issue of trust lightly. Not only are they trustworthy, but they expect others to be trustworthy as well. It's human nature to only expect of others that which we would do ourselves. If you are honest then you will expect others to be honest too. If you were a liar and a thief, it would be quite ridiculous to expect that others will not lie to you or steal from you. We only get in life what we give out, but that does not mean just because you are trustworthy you can trust them. Trust is something that I expect to receive so I give it.

To the people whom I truly love I expect it from them all the more. I give trust because I desire more intimacy. In life you never get what you want. **You only get what you inspect.** What you are not willing to inspect don't bother expecting. It is rather interesting that an airplane pilot still uses a checklist; despite the fact that he or she may have flown the same type of aircraft more than a thousand times. Why the need for such a thorough inspection? After all, the pilot has flown the same plane so many times that it should be second nature to fly safely to his destination.

The reason why he does the checklist is not because he doesn't trust himself. It is risk reward ratio. The pilot has much at stake. And what he can potentially lose from not inspecting is far too great to risk. He could lose innocent lives by ignoring the inspection process. It's very likely that if he or she doesn't go through every single item on their list that they will arrive at the destination safely. But just suppose there was one thing out of order on their checklist that they overlooked. What if there was frost on the engine, or a leaking valve that was overlooked? A seemingly minor oversight could cost the lives of many people. It's all about personal and corporate accountability.

Businesses can lose millions if not billions of dollars annually if they do not inspect their workers, their management, and the owners. When we say inspect we are not talking about calling people on the carpet when they have done something wrong. We are talking about simply comparing what was expected to what was done. Do you know what you expect? Do people know what you expect? When there is no clearness concerning expectations, that leads to mistrust. Inspecting is done before completion of a project, not after the fact.

I've heard people say things like, "I don't like a job where somebody is always looking over my shoulder." If you ever hear anyone say that, watch him or her closely. Generally people who say that, from my experience, are people who are sluggards, lazy, and try to beat the company out of money. It's not a crime to want to desire to work in an environment where you are not monitored daily. But quite honestly, you have to merit such a position. You don't just become a self-governed person after years of sloppy living.

If you want to get to the top, you manage your way to the top. The compassionate samurai gets promoted regularly, not through manipulation or coercion as some people choose. The compassionate samurai goes from one level to the next not by inspecting others under their command, but by first inspecting themselves. So you are not ready for promotion until you have first inspected yourself. And you aren't ready to inspect others until you first inspect yourself. One reason people fail to reach their goals of weight loss, financial independence, or even marital success is because they lack accountability.

Accountability is the tracking or accounting of results. Average people leave to chance those areas, falsely believing that they'll just work out in time. Even with yourself, you can't expect anything of you that you are not willing to inspect. A pilot checks frequently because then the corrections are small and easy. If you are off only a little bit but do not inspect for hours then when you do inspect you are so far off course it is too hard a correction and people give up.

Trust—an equitable right or interest in property distinct from the legal ownership of it: a property interest held by one person for the benefit of another.

According to the definition here a trust is held not for your own benefit but someone else's. The compassionate samurai lives his life thinking about the benefit of others not his own first. He maintains trust not for people to look on him and brag about how good and trusting he is, but rather for the benefit of another. There is so much at stake that other people will need to know that they can invest their trust in you, without having to worry about their decision.

When people have second thoughts about their decision to do business with you it could be a number of things that evokes their indecision. It could be buyer's remorse; they simply didn't see the value in parting with their money for your product. It could also be that the person is not trustworthy and because of that tends to distrust everyone else. Or it could be that you emitted a vibe that spells out distrust to them. Even in business one must always be more concerned about how the client benefits from the transaction not the seller of the services. Once you gain trust, keep it!

The High Price To Pay

The samurai takes the principle of trust to far extremes, and rightly so. There is always a high price to pay when trust is at stake. Some years ago, I was trying to obtain Chevron Corporation as a client. The deal looked favorable. What would have been the final piece to the puzzle was to be determined in a phone meeting that was supposed to be at a certain time. I was five minutes late for the conversation. The senior executive from Chevron told me that if he couldn't trust me to be on time and respect his time he certainly wasn't going to trust me with Chevron's money and he hung up.

We lost what would have been a very large contract over five minutes. We lost the potential contract because of loss of trust. I failed to earn it. Although upset, I understood what happened and made a resolve never to repeat the mistake of overlooking how each decision affects others trust in me. His actions toward me helped us to make millions of dollars since then. I learned a valuable lesson about trust. You may think to yourself, "You didn't even know that guy. How unfair! It was only five minutes."

This man trusted me to be on time for my phone conversation with him. This man had the power to make important decisions for Chevron involving large amounts of money and human resources. He had to have earned that trust along the way in his career with Chevron. As a steward of the company's resources he was demanding that I abide by the legal definition of trust. He had to look out for the better interest of his company by weeding out the very symptoms of distrust. The only barometer to measure my trustworthiness with him was by simply calling him when I said I would.

In his mind, I shouldn't even expect a second chance to prove myself at a greater level, when I failed on such a small level. There are always hidden costs and prices to pay when trust is breeched. Remember that. There is a very close relationship with trust and agreement. Broken agreements create broken trust. When you break your agreement with a person you have entered into a situation where that person may never enter an agreement with you again because you also broke trust with them.

A friend of mine, Dr. Aaron D. Lewis, a spiritual leader and writer, recently told me how he was asked to accompany his spiritual mentor Arch-Bishop LeRoy Bailey Jr. to New York City for a meeting with Bill Hybels. During the meeting, Aaron slipped away to purchase a car battery charger for his phone, since his battery was nearly dead. He walked around the corner to the New York Electronics Company to buy the charger, and the person in the store told him that the charger was sale priced at $69.95 if my friend had the cash.

He only had about $100.00 on him, and did not want to spend most of his cash on the charger, not knowing what he might need the remaining cash for later. There was nothing special about the charger to look at. It was just a regular car charger for a cell phone. The guy in the store started to tell my friend how this charger was special in that it could fully charge a car battery in less than twenty minutes. The package did not verify that what this guy was saying was true at all. As my friend was walking out the store and passing up the offer, the salesman yelled out, just give me $40.00 cash and take the charger.

Needing the charger, Dr. Lewis gave the man the money and went on his way. Later that day, Lewis went into a T-Mobile store to find out what a brand named T-Mobile phone charger should cost. To his surprise, the phone charger was priced at $19.95 for a brand name. He couldn't trust the salesman in the electronics store. Now you may be wondering to yourself, "What does it matter? In New York City they have so many tourists and millions of potential customers that it really doesn't matter about one person's business. Right?" Wrong.

The compassionate samurai is always concerned about contribution.
The compassionate samurai is not a taker but rather a giver.

The samurai is a long-term thinker. He or she thinks about the relationship not the immediate deal. One of the benefits of trust is relationship. Things like honor, respect, and trust, are long-term values. You can make money-selling drugs, but you are not contributing to humanity. The compassionate samurai is always concerned about contribution. The compassionate samurai is not a taker but rather a giver. If they are in a transaction they are always more concerned about how they can give rather than take away from the person with whom they are doing business.

The Value of Relationship

Trust is earned. So some people ask, "How can I trust someone that I don't even know?" Well, you don't have to know somebody in order to trust them. In fact, people are usually taken advantage of more by people whom they know than people they don't know at all. It starts with a decision. You trust others and you get relationship, Relationship will carry you through tough times. That's one of the benefits of trust. As you know, tough times will come.

The store manager of the electronics company in New York that intentionally overcharged my friend is probably overcharging several other people. When the time comes where they may not have as many customers to their store, they will suffer more severely than they have to. When you value relationship you know that those with whom you are in relationship with will always help to under gird you during tough times.

Joe Girad, the man who made it into the Guinness Book of World Records for selling more cars than any other salesman, did so by charging less and doing more volume. He could have tried to get more from one or two customers, but after he did that he would have lost those customers and perhaps many more because they would not have trusted him to get a good deal. He coined a term called the 250 rule. It says that the average person has a circle of people that they can influence of about 250 people.

So if you give great service you may increase by 250 people. If you offer horrible service you may decrease in business by 250 clients or sales, or maybe even more than that since bad news tends to travel faster than good news. I remember a very long time ago, maybe twenty years or so ago, I was downtown San Francisco and my Jaguar started steaming. I called (AAA) American Automobile Association road service. They asked me where did I want the car hauled to. Without pondering the thought I told the man haul it to Marin to a car mechanic that I have been dealing with for years.

The reason why I chose him and did not consider maybe 50 or more mechanics in between the distance from San Francisco to Marin is because of the trust I had in him. I know very little about car mechanics. On numerous previous occasions he could have easily charge me an extra few hundred dollars. He didn't. If I needed a six-dollar radiator cap: that's all that he sold me. We built a relationship over the years of trust. That's why I paid several hundred dollars to tow it 35 miles instead of going to someone I didn't know, 2 blocks away for free.

One of the industry niches our company serves is network marketing and home based businesses. It is an industry that in the past has been known for exaggeration. People will make exaggerated promises of how much money can be made for almost no work. It is a great industry and like any other business you must work. When people make exaggerated claims they may enroll more people initially, but no relationship is built because of the lack of trust and they can't maintain it.

When the truth is always spoken, including the not so pleasant aspects, a relationship is built on trust. These teams stay together through thick and thin for very long periods of time. This happens on the church speaking circuit also. If a big time preacher or speaker agrees to speak at a smaller church or venue, and later receives an offer from a much larger church they can be tempted to cancel the smaller church. That has a larger immediate benefit but carries a huge back end price. In time, not only will that person lose the trust of the person who invited them, but they will not get as many engagements overall, as people talk and they will consider them a bad risk.

Does Competency Overrule Trust?

Sometimes people believe that competency overrules trust or arrogantly believe they don't need trust. For example, in the world of sports we often see favors lent to athletes with above average athletic skills. From college days, maybe even high schools years on, teachers and professors will help athletes to pass on to the next grade level although they really don't have a concrete grasp on the work. They get the favors because they are skilled on the court or field, yet their other-life may not be so trustworthy. Some people overlook this but such overlooking cannot last forever.

For example there is a phenomenal athlete by the name of Terrel Owens. He is quite an amazing wide receiver, perhaps the best in the country. He played for the San Francisco 49ers for nearly five years. He missed key meetings, showed up late, and pretty much had an attitude that he needed to be treated special. Trust eroded and despite his talent he was given away. He promised to go to the Baltimore Ravens, and at the last minute reneged so that he could get a bigger contract for more money with the Philadelphia Eagles.

Then he played less than two years before they released him. Now he is with the Dallas Cowboys and things are already shaky. He is on the verge of no team ever wanting to take him on. Eventually, regardless of how competent his skills are, unless he changes, he will not have a place to go. What happens after he is no longer able to play the game, because he is just too old? Who will share opportunities with him? It may very well be possible that his riches may turn into vapor.

Don't mistake what I am saying. I don't wish badness on him or anyone for that matter. I hope he has a wonderfully enjoyable career, and a long-lasting one. I am simply trying to convey the message that trust is not something to take lightly because the road back from trust can be a very long, tiresome, and lonely one. Think prevention, and develop trust habits now that will become your character for now and forever. Do the little things that build trust and receive huge pay offs down the road.

The Road Back From Breeching Trust

It would be pretty disappointing if we were to end this entire section without offering some hope. There is hope if you have been in a situation where your trust has been compromised and you failed those that trusted you. First though, realize that everybody is not going to extend trust to you again. Some people are just going to shut you out for life, that's just the way it is. That's a high price that you sometimes have to pay for breeching trust.

Others may forgive you and allow you another chance to rebuild with them. But I can tell you this much, if you choose to burn someone twice in a serious way, you might as well hang it up for life. Your name will become so marred after awhile that no one will want to deal with you at all. And when that happens you will be left in a most vulnerable state. You need the help, assistance, protection, and love of other people. Simply put, you need other people's support. So here are two things that you need to do to rebuild your trust with someone that you have lost it with.

How To Repair Trust

I. **Start making commitments and keeping them!** There is power in commitment. When you make a commitment you bind your-self to your word, and when you keep your commitment you earn trust. You are no more than your word, so start keeping it.

Start small and build up, no different than lifting weights. You don't start off lifting three hundred pounds. You build up to it. It is the same with trust. Start with small agreements and keep pushing yourself to larger ones.

2. **Making yourself accountable to someone else.** The higher you are in authority the easier it is to not make yourself accountable, especially to the people with less authority. I believe that you ought to make yourself accountable to those on the higher and on the lower ends of the chain. Accountability gives you an ability to have more in your account. It's the only way to have lasting increase in your life, and it's the safest way also.

A compassionate samurai has the capacity to trust others and themselves with their life and have the wisdom to know when to do so.

Compassionate Samurai ask "how can I?"

Average people ask "Can I?"

You can't afford poverty. —Unknown

Chapter Eight

Abundance

Abundance—Overflowing like wave after wave

In books that deal with prosperity, chapters that deal with money and abundance are usually not listed first. There is a very good reason for this. Before you can understand abundance you really need to be prepared. You need a foundation on which to build. People tend to jump over all of the other chapters and go straight to the chapter that they believe will release them from their prison of debt and poverty. The real truth is that the reason they are in the prison of indebtedness in the first place is because they have played their entire life the same way that they read those books. They skip over everything.

Be Willing To Pay The Price

One of the first pieces of an abundant mindset is to be willing to pay the price. There is no free lunch. Certainly there are faster more effective ways to do things, but a compassionate samurai is willing to invest time, money, effort, even failure in order to create whatever it is they want. Average people look for the easy way and attempt to skip steps. Things that are necessary for them to know and understand in life, they refute, not realizing that it is those things that are much needed to pass onto the next level. You can't skip the basics and expect to move on to the intermediate level.

It just doesn't work like that. There are people that dream of buying hotel buildings yet don't even own a home. It's very difficult to buy a hotel if you've never owned any real property. First things must come first. I did not say it was impossible. All things are possible. It's just highly improbable. Look around. Average people want to achieve great success but yet avoid the necessary steps toward attaining such a goal. "I want to be the owner of a multi-billion dollar corporation." That goal is a very lofty one. Yes, it is attainable.

But then the average person wants to bypass spending years learning about finances or going to seminars to learn about people skills. In managing a small several million dollar a year business you start learning the lessons of cashflow and succession planning or holding context of culture as your number of employees rapidly expands. The point is that abundance does not just happen. It happens in stages and in steps. Some of the best training I personally received as a facilitator was when I volunteered to do home party presentations to market seminars for my mentor.

It wasn't simply presentation skills or content I learned. I dealt with, and learned to connect with, the most resistant people, who had never heard of his seminars, and felt forced to hear when I began sharing about them. I learned to deal with the most adverse conditions, like a baby screaming while I was presenting, and how to predict and head problems off ahead of time. None of this did I get paid for. These lessons I have applied thousands of times in my career as a facilitator. Other people felt that volunteering was either beneath them or just didn't want to spend the time.

They just wanted to be a facilitator. They never made it. They wanted to jump to the top rung of the ladder without climbing the bottom rungs. I was willing to pay the price to be where I was years ago as a facilitator let alone where I am now. A very dear friend of mine, Lance Giroux, myself and our wives, traveled to Hong Kong 20 years ago. At one point during the trip, he wanted to exchange money. It seemed there were money exchange stores every fifty yards downtown. I recommended that he not go and exchange any money.

He asked, "Why not?" I replied, "Because all the signs say no commission charged, no sales fee. When something looks like a free lunch and you don't know the price, the real price is usually too high." As an experiment he exchanged only a hundred dollar bill. He received approximately $84 back. They took 16%!! They simply called the fee something else. *There is a price for everything.* Know the price and based on the reward or benefit decide if it is worth paying. If it is worth paying the time, money or energy, then be willing to pay the price.

Another version of the average person not being willing to pay the price is the old adage, "Don't step over a dollar to pick up a dime." That's a waste of good time and a way to regress with regards to abundance. The abundant thinker does not mind putting out in order to get more back. I've heard people complain about the fees that some financial planners charge. They may charge as high as $4000.00 to $5000.00 for consultation. Occasionally someone who has not done our seminars will make a comment that our seminars or books and CD's are too expensive.

Are the financial planners fees or our seminars fee too high? That answer all depends on what kind of service you receive from your investment. It's one of the reasons we measure results and publish them on our web site.

People pay anywhere from $400-$800 currently for our weekend Personal Mastery seminar. If they are in a home based business or direct sales, the average person, based on surveyed results, increases their income $352 a month from what they made previously. In a year, that's a return of $4224 on $400-$800 investment.

That's a 500% or 1000% return. Compassionate samurai doesn't sit around counting pennies when he could be counting 100-dollar bills. Compassionate samurai are willing to pay for experts who truly can make a difference in all areas of their life whether it is a good financial planner, a good tax strategist, a good real estate broker, a nutritionist, health coach or relationships expert. You pay them to be a part of your system to see what you may not be privy to. I've used a planner to do a financial plan for me, a *13b1.*

Before abundance manifests in a tangible way in your life,
it must first manifest in your mind.

Without getting too technical, a *13b1* is a pension plan investment in the stock market where you don't lose when the stock market goes down and you gain 60% of the increase. I use it as a portion of a conservative base to my investment portfolio. During the stock market crashes of 2000—2002 it saved me well into 6 figures. I would never have even heard about this type of investment if I hadn't been willing to pay the financial planner their well-deserved fee. Average people try and save a few dollars by doing it themselves. Pay the professionals well, and learn enough to ask the right questions.

Before abundance manifests in a tangible way in your life, it must first manifest in your mind. If abundance never takes root there, then you will probably never experience it. So if you are one of the ones that skipped all of the previous necessary chapters leading up to this one, stop now, and start this book from the beginning. Read the introduction. Do it now! If you've already passed that point, then it's all right for you to pass go. Let's move forward and condition your mind for abundance.

The Scarcity Mindset

Let's approach abundance from it's opposite. There is something that is called the scarcity mindset. Scarcity is the position that there is never enough and it is usually based on the position that the person believes that they are not enough. The average person looks around and sees nearly 7 billion people on the planet and thinks I am only one person. I am not enough. Then they have various experiences in life that validate they are not enough. They don't do well enough in school or aren't able to make a friend or keep their parents together. Then they look outside of themselves and say:

- There are not enough customers.
- There are not enough good men or women.
- There is not enough time.
- There is not enough money.
- There is not enough oil.
- There is not enough love.
- There is not enough_____. You fill in the blank.

A compassionate samurai realizes that *your wholeness and completeness does not depend on any external circumstances.* Brand that in your brain. That is our definition

131

of *abundance.* That is a very different definition for abundance than the way most people define it. The average person thinks abundance is a certain amount of income or net worth. Some great philosophers like Buckminister Fuller define it as the number of days you can go without working and not decrease your lifestyle. Those are fine definitions, but ours is a fundamentally different approach.

Abundance is the position that your wholeness and completeness
is not dependent on external circumstances.

Abundance is the position that your wholeness and completeness is not dependent on external circumstances. Your wholeness and completeness is from birth because of your spiritual nature and your connection to God. Since God is infinite, you being connected to Him are complete. In addition, your wholeness and completeness depends totally on what is on the inside of you, nothing else. If you do not have anything on the inside of you, (meaning character) you will be forced to live a life of always proving your worth through the attainment of things. That is, in fact, where the average person seeks their validation-outside themselves in friends, their titles or job, and material wealth.

Haven't you noticed the number of people who are on an endless chase of accumulating more without being happy? When a person tries to use material things to fill that hole of satisfaction it is never enough. It is no different than an addiction. There are people who drive Rolls Royce cars and

Bentleys, yet are poor spiritually, mentally, emotionally, and yes financially. They continue to rob good ole' Peter, and never even pay Paul. Some people are living one deal away from foreclosure and auto repossession. That's a scarcity mindset. I know of people that have to change their car every year so that onlookers might think that they are doing well off in life. That's scarcity thinking. Some people can't keep a stable address, they move from here to there, from the West Coast to the East Coast, from New England to Florida and so on. They are making new moves seemingly every year. Not always, but many times they are "running" looking for something outside themselves to fill a hole of dissatisfaction. They have not distinguished where there satisfaction comes from as separate from the "more, better, different" realm.

One of the challenges with Amercia as a whole today is that the average person is looking for satisfaction in the material realm. Hence their emptiness. Other countries looking in see the United States's great material wealth and they mistakenly link wealth to spiritual bankruptcy. The compassionate samurai is clear where there satisfaction comes from and then chooses to play the more better different game to create, but never looks for their validation in the realm of more because that is an endless game. Seeking satisfaction in that realm becomes an addiction.

Another example of scarcity mindset is when a person has to work all of the time, and can never take a day off. That person believes that they can't afford to lose a days pay. Maybe they won't lose a days pay, yet they still falsely believe that things cannot function without their presence. That too is scarcity thinking. I've seen people that have a six-figure income, live in palatial homes, and drive luxury cars, yet if their wife asks them to spend time with the family for a weekend they cannot. They work all of the time, make tons of money, and yet won't enjoy it with the people they love. In their minds they believe that if they stop working their brook will dry up. That is not true, but some people believe that anyway. Scarcity mindset can manifest in many different ways. You can have a scarcity mindset with or without money. The abundance mindset must precede the manifestation of prosperity in health, relationships or finances for it to last. Recently on the front page of AOL there was a story of a man who had won the lottery in 2002. Today, in 2007, he is totally broke, according to the article. Now before you begin thinking that this man lost a measly $5 million dollars, think again. He won $315 million dollars in 2002 and today has nothing to show for it. You go and figure that one out. He claims that people stole his money. Even if that were true, I am sure that you would agree that $315 million dollars is a whole lot of money to steal. The real deal here is that this man had scarcity mentality. If he had abundance mentality he would have created more abundance with his fortune. Because his mind was not conditioned for that kind of money he really did not know what to do with it once he received it. That is usually the case of many Power Ball or lottery ticket winners. It is the subconcious thinking and character that must change first.

Your thoughts are invariably what will always create wealth in your life. And, it is your thoughts that create the right habits that facilitate perpetual wealth.

You've heard the phrase "money makes money." That's not always true. Abundance thinking creates money. Your thoughts are invariably what will always create wealth in your life. And, it is your thoughts that create the right habits that facilitate perpetual wealth. It's obvious that this man who won $315 million dollars did not think like a person that would normally have that kind of money. And because he didn't think like a mega multi-millionaire, the money fell through his hands. His scarcity thoughts reduced his net worth right back down to the place where it identically matched his thoughts. What is your thinking like? Do you have a problem with other people's prosperity? Samurai's are never concerned about what other people have. That is another reflection of scarcity thinking.

For Consciousness Sake

A compassionate samurai learns to conquer the subconcious mind before the circumstance. The average person is always trying to overcome the circumstance. In the area of finances my mentor taught me a major lesson on conquering scarcity thinking amidst tough financial times. It was in the late 70's and his seminar company was not doing well. In fact they were in debt, several hundred thousand dollars in overdue bills, losing about $70,000 every month. In the midst of all of this, Tom pulls me aside and says, "We need to buy a new car. I need to make a statement to my subconscious mind that even though we are losing money I am still powerful enough to turn this thing around." At times consolidation, and cut backs, are necessary. But more than not, training your mind to not buy into the present reality is far better. Compassionate samurai anchor their vision and let reality adjust. Average people anchor in reality and let their vision adjust. Your mind only produces that which it focuses on. If you focus on the debt of the company then you will inevitably get more indebted. Beliefs are changed by repetition and emotional involvement. Having a new Lincoln Town car at several hundred dollars a month would not change our circumstance, but it can change your head.

My first thought was, "What'll the employees think?" I was having people hold their checks and not cash them immediately. He said, "That's why we are not buying a Rolls Royce. We could. But that is too far outside the zone and we would get more resistance than I want to handle at the moment." Buying a car while in debt was so counter-intuitive for me at that time in my life. Tom did turn the company around. Years later when the company was doing very well he bought a Rolls Royce. I still remember graduates complaining. After the event with the Lincoln Town car I never begrudged whatever he spent money on as I realized how important it was to keep his head straight. We all had jobs because of it. Buying the Lincoln Town car changed his thinking and it actually forced good times to come into existence. It also taught me to consider people's reactions, but never be victim to that.

Now, this won't work for everybody. Why? Because you respond to stimuli different. This is VERY important. There are people who go out and buy expensive things, put themselves in huge debt, thinking this is wealth consciousness. No. Tom responded to having a Lincoln Town car by thinking of himself as wealthy. It is what he needed to work on at that time. He was already tithing. At one point in my life I was learning about tithing and made the commitment to do so. That required us selling one of our two nice cars and buying an old green station wagon for six hundred dollars. With no car payments that allowed us to tithe. Other people working with my mentor accused me of lacking wealth consciousness. My understanding of Tom and abundance was that tithing was a fundamental principle of abundance. Later on in life, long after he had died, the company was in very uncertain times. Many of us did not know if we would have a job. I didn't know if I wanted to stay and had no idea what I would do if I left. Economics were challenging. I went out and bought a very nice used Jaguar SJS sports car because of my lesson with Tom and the Town car. At that point in my life I was tithing and it was a different issue I had to work on my subconscience with. I was affirming that I was capable of making life work no matter what the circumstance. It worked. There are times when what you do may not seem to have a rhyme or reason to the people who are watching you. A compassionate samurai doesn't worry about that. A compassionate samurai lives their life by principles

Tithing—Practice of Abundance

Tithing is the practice of giving away the first tenth of your income to wherever you receive your spiritual guidance, your church, temple or synagogue. For the moment, put aside the spiritual aspect and let's look at this from strictly an abundance perspective. How do you change belief systems? They are changed by repetition and emotional involvement. The more emotion involved the less repetition is needed. The less emotion the more repetition is required.

The average person suffers from a scarcity mindset and the consequent behavior is to "hold onto," whether it is love, money, time, or whatever. Imagine every time you receive a check you immediately write a check for 10% of that to your church, synagogue, or temple. Can you feel the internal conflict a person with scarcity mindset would go through? That's emotional involvement. How often do you receive income checks? Weekly, Bi-monthly, monthly? That's repetition.

Perhaps you are thinking, "yes, but I know people who tithe that are not well off financially. Why?" I wondered the same question, especially after it worked so well in my own life. That's because there are other principles also involved. In the Old Testament a prophet named Malachi said

"Bring all the tithes into the store house that there may be food in My house, and prove me now in this, says the Lord of hosts, If I will not open for you the windows of heaven and pour out for you such blessing that there will not be room enough to receive it." Malachi 3:10

If you want to do your own research, it's an easy one to find, as it is the last book in the Old Testament. Another principle or character trait already covered in this book is *Personal Responsibility*. Tithing puts us in a position to be blessed, but we are still responsible to do our part and walk through the door. Some people tithe and think money will just drop on their head. Tithing is the beginning and it is a great way to combat scarcity thinking.

From a spiritual perspective you give this to where you get your spiritual nourishment because it is acknowledging God as the source not you. Giving to good causes such as Cancer Society or Girl Scouts is an offering on top of tithing. From a strictly financial perspective every act of giving, no matter where it is given, combats scarcity thinking.

Receiving—The Hidden Obstacle To Abundance

One of the keys to abundance is your ability to receive. The average person does not have the capacity to receive abundance. How could that be a problem? Receiving is easy you think? Not so. Imagine you had a common water glass. Imagine someone starts pouring the ocean into your water glass. Would it matter that you had the whole ocean pouring into your glass? You can only keep what the glass will hold. The average person needs to increase the size of their glass.

I had a pastor ask me to coach him around finances. I asked if he tithed. He chuckled and said, "Of course". I knew him to be a giver, but it can be surprising who does not tithe. Then I asked if he invested 10% in himself. His eyebrows became furrowed. He asked for further clarification. I asked, "Do you take the second tenth of what you earn and invest it in stocks, real estate, or something that is for the sole purpose of increasing your net worth? He said he had never been able to do that.

He gave to his church, to his children, to friends, to strangers, but he never gave to himself. He hadn't worked on his ability to receive. When you give to yourself you are changing what your sub-conscious says about you. It starts saying you are wealthier. It says you are a worthy person. If you believe you are born in God's image, then you are a king. A compassionate samurai is totally okay with receiving. They feel worthy of it. Average people don't feel worthy of receiving.

When I bought my first Jaguar I remember feeling embarrassed about driving it. My feeling of unworthiness was battling against me. Give an average person a compliment and they say' "It was nothing," or "I bought it in a consignment shop." A compassionate samurai says, "Thank you." Give an average person something and they reply, "I can't take that."

Humility is, understanding that God is the source not you.

Average people confuse humility, which is a good thing, with a poor self-image. Humility is, understanding that God is the source not you. He is the ocean with infinite water willing to pour into you. You are worthy of the finer things in life. Make a practice of spending time and money on you. It is not selfish as long as it is balanced with the giving.

Getting A System In Place

This is why in the financial realm the system of 10-10-80 works so well. A compassionate samurai gives the first tenth to the place of their spiritual nourishment, the second tenth they invest and never spend. The remaining 80% is what pays all your expenses including taxes, groceries, the car and whatever offerings you decide to give. A compassionate samurai increases the first two categories as they grow, always keeping the giving and investing at the same percentage. They continually are better off living on a smaller and smaller percentage.

This systematic practice of giving and receiving (investing) activates the power of compounding interest. Most people are familiar with the principle and yet few implement it. Investing $100 a month at 16% interest accumulates to over a ten million dollars in 40 years. Average people are myopic. They look only at the immediate impact. Average people think, "$100 won't change anything." They might look a year out and they will say, "$1200 won't change anything." The average person doesn't see how the power of compounding interest can create them 10 million dollars.

The same is true with time. With just thirty minutes of writing, five days a week, you could be an accomplished author in less than six months time. It just takes discipline. Systems leverage your time, money and abilities. Systems are tools that create abundance. You have to have a system in place if you want to live in abundance. First off, abundance is not so much something that you find yourself living in, as it is a principle by which you live by. If you live by the principle of abundance you will experience abundance.

There are things that you have to do, and they must become a part of your character if you are going to be abundant. The traditional samurai was always frugal, not cheap. Frugality or valuing the worth of things is a wonderful system to live by. It will always ensure that you are not overspending and being unnecessarily wasteful. Having a budget or a plan for how you allocate your income is a system. Average people don't have a system nor do they follow it. Compassionate samurai have a budget no matter how much money they earn. It is a way of thinking.

The system operates like a flight path in determining where to come back to. Systems do not box you in. They create flexibility. One system we have in Klemmer & Associates is that if four weeks before a trip someone's flight is not booked; they get an email reminding them so that we get the best fares. In the busy world we live in it would be easy periodically for different people to book at the last minute. That little system conservatively saves us more than $25,000 a year. What systems can you put in place to enhance your life?

Being Solution Oriented

One of the keys to abundance is having a solution-oriented mindset. The average person although they think of themselves as positive, is not solution oriented. As I was writing this chapter, a moderately successful interior decorator came to our house. We started talking about what I do for a living. I gave her some books and she was very excited. I mentioned a seminar we were holding locally in a few weeks. Instantly, she said, "I'd like to, but I can't because I work Saturday's." She had an average mindset not that of a compassionate samurai.

Average people ask themselves, "Can I do this?" and they base it on the circumstances they see. This woman looked at her schedule in her mind, and when she asked the question, "Can I?" she came up negative. *An abundant thinker asks different questions.* An abundant thinker asks, "How can I?" This simple twist in asking a different question changes everything. It forces your mind to create a solution. If this woman had asked herself, "How could I attend," her subconscious would have immediately begun searching for an answer.

In our Personal Mastery seminar we do an exercise where everyone crosses the room using a different mechanism. One walks. Perhaps the next crawls, the next person dances across. Eventually someone will get stuck and go, "I don't know what to do." We never force anyone to do anything, but amazing things usually start to happen. When you say, "I don't know what to do," all you are saying is that your conscious mind doesn't know what to do. That is the smallest part of you. Yet the average person is totally victim, to their conscious mind. That's all they are aware of. Your subconscious can solve hundreds of problems, your conscious mind can't.

A compassionate samurai is not reasonable. Average people are reasonable. Reason resides in your conscious mind. Reason has a very important function, but it is not to solve problems. Reason looks at circumstances and your past. All a person's past tells them is what beliefs they were operating from. It has nothing to do with what was possible because you can change beliefs. The conscious mind is the smallest part of you. At this point in the exercise, everyone is usually cheering the person on that is stuck. Our facilitator will pull a $100.00 bill out of their wallet and give them 30 seconds from when they stop talking to come up with a unique way across the room.

Within seconds an idea hits them. They get across. There are many points to the exercise, but the one to focus on right now is "How many ways are there across the room?" There are infinite ways across the room. There is always a way. Average people however have scarcity thinking and think there is one way to do anything. One way to buy a house, one way to sell, one way to get promoted, one way to talk with your children. The average person is worried about finding the way.

Quit worrying about it. The next time you are stuck, think of this exercise and think like a compassionate samurai. There are an infinite number of ways even when they are not visible to you. A solution might involve people you don't know, but have access to. The solution might involve money that is not in your possession or visible to you. A solution might involve knowledge you don't have and can't see. A compassionate samurai forces himself or herself to look for a solution by asking, "How can I?"

Super Size That Please

If there is always a solution, how big are you willing to think? Average people think small. Average people think about what their eyes and ears tell them. Compassionate samurai just naturally super size it and ask, "How can I increase this by 10 times?" I once had a conversation with Tom Schrieter who is an icon in the home-based business industry. He is a best-selling author, a giver, and a multi-millionaire. I asked, "Tom, you are a best selling author and I too have a best selling book, called _If How To's Were Enough We Would All Be Skinny Rich and Happy_." What would you do with my book? He replied, "How many do you sell at the back of the room sales?" "Typically I would do a few hundred," I answered.

He said, "Start thinking about selling 10,000 in a sale instead." I asked, "How would I sell 10,000 at a time?" He said start with me and we cranked out a deal on the spot. Within two months I made two more 10,000-book sales with other people! I started looking at selling them by the box to achievers so I started making a lot of 100 book sales. The possibilities were there all along, I just wasn't thinking big enough.

A friend of mine who is a real live compassionate samurai, Bob Harrison (www.increase.org), is called Dr. Increase because of who he is and what he attracts through his teaching. He bought a mansion for a dollar and with no monthly payments. Yes, it's more complicated than that, but it's true. Check his office out, they'll tell you the whole story if you want. It started with an ad he read that said, "No reasonable offer refused." He thought to himself, if they won't refuse a reasonable offer, maybe they wouldn't refuse an unreasonable offer!

He was thinking much bigger than his finances at the moment. Average people won't go looking for huge deals or even allow themselves to dream of the possibilities. What would it be like for you to earn twice what you are currently earning? What would it be like for you to raise a million dollars for a cause you believe in? What would it be like for you to have a job you were twice as excited about going to each morning? Can you take a current dream and double it? Can you multiply that by ten?

Yo-yo Thoughts of The Average

We have talked extensively of scarcity thinking that afflicts the average person. There are some people who are so imbedded in it they live in poverty whether times are good or bad. There are others, compassionate samurai who live in abundance no matter what the economic times look like. In fact, frequently, more millionaires are made during depressions than in great economic times. The vast majority of people, however, ride a yo-yo with their prosperity and all areas of their life, goes up and down.

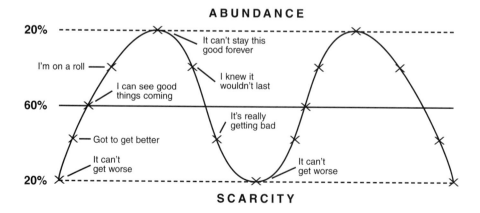

Start any where on the graph. Average people are thinking it has got to get better. It gets slightly better. They are thinking, "See, I knew it would get better." It gets better. Then "Good times are just ahead." Then they start thinking, "I can't imagine it getting any better." Their success starts to level off. Then they start thinking, "Good things don't last forever." All good things must come to an end". Their results start to slip. "I knew it couldn't go on like this forever." It starts getting worse. "Oh this is bad." It gets worse. "This is terrible. It can't get any worse." They bottom out. "It can't stay this way forever. It has got to get better." Then start the climb again.

There is no lack. There is more than enough. You are more than enough.
Thus there is an abundant supply of everything you need!

The truly abundant mindset is never swayed by the economy, so-called recessions, or even inflation. The abundant mindset is always well grounded in the reality that if abundance does not seem to exist, then I'll have to create it. They realize that the universe has more than enough resources to go around, enough to make everybody happy and full. So there is never a reason to be covetous or envious of another person. If you can't handle other people having great amounts of money without feeling feelings of jealousy then you have a scarcity mentality.

There is no lack. There is more than enough. You are more than enough. Thus there is an abundant supply of everything you need! As a compassionate samurai you must build a character of abundance. It must live deep inside you so that you don't have to think. Whether circumstances are good or bad, whether you are riding high or low, you think abundance. You are going to be taking life on. Look for challenging problems to solve. Sooner or later these challenges will squeeze you. It is at that time that all these character traits including abundance will come out. When you squeeze an orange, juice comes out because that it what was inside. When life squeezes you, greatness will come out.

"You can't afford poverty." —Unknown

Abundance

Compassionate Samurai ask what will happen if I don't take this risk.

Average people ask what happens if I fail.

"Courage is the first of human qualities because it is the quality which guarantees the others." —Aristotle

Chapter Nine

Boldness

One isn't necessarily born with courage, but one is born with potential. Without courage, we cannot practice any other virtue with consistency. We can't be kind true, merciful, generous, or honest.—Maya Angelou *(in USA Today, 5 March 1988)*

What do you think of when you think of courage? A small child may immediately think of a lion as a symbol of strong courage and gallantry since many of us were taught that the lion is the king of the jungle. Even in the famous children's book written by L. Frank Baum from 1900, *The Wonderful Wizard of Oz*, which was later, adapted into a MGM movie in 1939, *The Wizard of Oz*, depicts the Lion character that should have courage, as missing it. As the movie unfolds he discovers he always had it, it was just that he didn't display it.

Fear had so crippled his ability to see himself for who he actually was, that he lived his life acting out his alter ego as a frightened coward rather than a brave beast that all of the other animals should have feared. It is somewhat of an automatic assumption that lions are simply supposed to possess dauntless faith no matter what the obstacles are. *The Lion King*, the third highest grossing animated feature film ever released in the United States, and one of the most prolific and successful Broadway shows ever, depicts Mufasa, king of the pride lands and his progeny Simba, the young heir to his throne.

Mufasa was an extremely courageous lion, and protector of his family and land. However, his boldness and courage were not easily transferred to his son Simba because he was still in the school of learning the truth about courage. After each lesson taught, his uncle Scar would immediately seek to undo everything that his father taught him, by instilling fear in the young lion. Perhaps you may not have realized it, but you too are a lion, at least symbolically speaking. You have the courage, but are you displaying it?

Are you more like Mufasa, or Simba as we see at the beginning of the movie? The average person doesn't take risks and they know it. They choose comfort and security over opportunity. The average person is in a job they don't like and they do it because they think they have to, afraid to change. The average person is in a relationship and they are afraid to bring certain topics up. The average person perhaps goes to church but will not voice his or her questions and doubts because they are afraid of being judged and ostracized.

The average people in business is afraid to give up any control and is trying to do it all themself. They are like the lion in the Wizard of Oz trembling and looking somehow to find the courage they think they have lost. *The good news is that you have it!* Just like the lion of Oz or Simba in the Lion King you already have it. Don't celebrate just yet. You too will have the challenges that the lion in the Wizard of Oz and Simba in The Lion King faced *so that you might display courage.*

Like they did, you will have to come face to face with some hard-hitting realities about yourself. One such reality is that you are a warrior that is called to win major battles in life. However, adversities and obstacles are bound to come. When that happens, how do you respond? Do you run for cover or do you run towards danger knowing that you have the innate ability to overcome any obstruction that may come your way?

For the compassionate samurai, courage is not something
they display every now and then, but rather something that
they showcase every moment of their life.

Compassionate samurai eat problems for breakfast, lunch and supper. They do it for fun. They see it as part of who they are. They look at every problem as a set of weights to grow stronger. For the compassionate samurai, courage is not something they display every now and then, but rather something that they showcase every moment of their life.

Danger—Your Opportunity To Awaken Courage

For most people, different events have occurred throughout their life that have fooled them into thinking they don't have courage. Courage lies asleep quietly until awakened by an opportunity to confront danger head on. A compassionate samurai looks for danger as an opportunity to awaken their courage. In Thailand several years ago there was a beautiful statue of Buddha in the middle of town. Due to some construction they needed to move it. It turned out to be much heavier than they thought. They hooked the statue up to chains and vehicles to move it and under the pressure it cracked.

They became aware that it was a solid gold Buddha that have been plastered over and then nicely painted. It had sat there for literally several hundred years with no one aware that there was a solid gold Buddha inside the nicely painted one. Apparently, years before, a warring tribe was about to overtake the village, the villagers wanted to protect their gold statue but couldn't move it in time. Their solution was to cover it up and paint it. It worked! That's much like you and I.

Events in our life where we were not acting out as the lions we were born to be covered up the real us. For some people they have gotten so covered up they have even forgotten they were lions, much less that they should possess courage. The key to revealing the gold statue inside was the applied pressure of the chains when they tried to move it. Compassionate samurai see pressure as a good thing. It is the opportunity to see the beauty inside and awaken the sleeping character of courage.

Low Self-Esteem And Courage

Sometimes low self-esteem is connected to a lack of courage. We fail in business, we fail in school, we get turned down for a date, or we overeat and see ourselves as weak. The list goes on. Our interpretation of events claims that we lack courage (read the chapter, Facts Are Meaningless, in my book When Good Intentions Run Smack Into Reality). If low self-esteem can be directly correlated to a lack of goodly courage, then having courage would then be the recognition of one's own potential. It is when you discover your own potential and worth in life that you are able to confront every enemy seeking to dissuade you from tapping into that potential. The person who does not realize their potential is typically bound by fear—fear of the unknown. That fear usually handicaps one's ability to fight forward, leaving them in a worthless position. Let's look at the definition in Webster's Dictionary.

Courage—the attitude of facing and dealing with anything recognized as dangerous, difficult, or painful, instead of withdrawing from it; quality of being fearless or brave; valor

Courage is the attitude of confronting danger or even your greatest fear. In the famous bible story of David and Goliath, I am not convinced that David was born with the courage to fight a giant that all of his predecessors feared greatly. In fact, in many translations of the Bible it says that when Goliath appeared, everyone ran. Everyone would include David, wouldn't it? It would include the king. It would even include the men chosen to be on the front row for that day. Imagine that. Here are veteran soldiers trained and prepared to die and they were afraid!

Courage is not the absence of fear. To do something when you are oblivious of the risks involved is not courage. Courage is acting in the face of fear. It is looking fear in the eye and spitting in its face. If you have fear, welcome to the human race. The minute you care there is fear. That's okay. It's natural. It is a scary world to raise children in no matter what kind of neighborhood you live in. With divorce rates at 50% of all marriages it makes marriage a scary venture.

With the majority of all businesses failing it is normal to be afraid to start your own business. Growing old with diminished physical capacity is scary. If you are not afraid you are smoking dope. In fact, then you are still afraid, you have just covered up those feelings of fear. What comes next is courage. Courage is a type of response to fear. David was afraid, but eventually stood up to Goliath. What helped him display his courage?

1. David practiced courage before he got to Goliath.

2. David kept rewards in front of his face.

3. David used a support group

4. David capitalized on his strengths rather than copy someone else.

5. David used his connection to God, infinite, to overshadow the fear of his eyes and ears.

Regardless of your faith, this is a great story to learn from. Take the time to read it in Samuel 1:17.

1. Practice

David combated his low self-esteem with practice. He was a shepherd boy. How many times have we asked ourselves who am I to do this? David kills a bear and a lion before he kills Goliath. He worked his way up in courage. Sometimes people try and skip rungs on the ladder and reach right for the top. If you own a home, but do not have an investment property the idea is not to take every penny of your equity and roll it on your first deal. Kill a bear first. Take a portion of your equity and do a small deal. Do another medium deal.

Eventually you may build your courage where you can roll it all on a spectacular opportunity. If you are widowed or simply have not dated in years, killing a bear might not even be going on a date, but simply going out in a group of mixed single company. The firemen who we all see as heroic, who climbed stairs in a building collapsing and on fire during the tragedy of September 11, 2001, had practiced entering buildings on fire so many times, they saw it as simply doing their job. If there is a fear that is preventing you from moving on with what really matters to you in life, practice confronting it. Don't confront foolishly but with goodly demeanor and systematically.

Even failure still requires courage. Everyone knows Michael Jordan and how he was a clutch basketball player. Here is what he said:

"I've missed more than 9000 shots in my career. I've lost almost 300 games. 26 times, I've been trusted to take the game winning shot and missed. I've failed over and over and over again in my life. And that is why I succeed." —Michael Jordan

We live in a society that frowns on and condemns the person who fails in life. One of the things that people fail to realize is that no one ever becomes a success in life without having had multiple failures first. Simply because you have failed at something does not mean you are a failure. Who would call Michael Jordan a failure? Thomas Edison had many failures before he made his light bulb work, and had significantly more failure after he pioneered that great invention. Colonel Saunders, the famous founder of Kentucky Fried Chickens famous recipe, had dozens of jobs that he was fired from before he started KFC and made a multi-million dollar success.

A compassionate samurai practices climbing out on the limb until it breaks.
Then they dust themselves off and do it again.

My mentor called me into his office a few weeks after I was working for him. He asked, "What has been your biggest failure here in the first few weeks?" I pondered a moment thinking maybe I had done something wrong that I was unaware of. Then, with nothing coming to my mind, I proudly stated I hadn't made any mistakes. He said, "Oh. We have a serious problem. You need to know I have never fired anyone for making a mistake, even someone who made a $100,000 failure. But I have fired people for not risking. If you haven't failed then you must not have risked enough. Your assignment is to make the biggest failure you can in the next two weeks."

I was shell-shocked. My whole life had been avoiding failure. He wasn't telling me to purposely fail. He was telling me to risk until I failed. All the fruit of life is out on the tree limb and the average person is clinging to the tree trunk. A compassionate samurai practices climbing out on the limb until it breaks. Then they dust themselves off and do it again. They become a professional limb walker. Practice! Become numb or neutral on failure. Courage is a maximum gain strategy.

2. Rewards Are Okay

In the story of David and Goliath, David inquired as to what the reward would be for killing Goliath. He was promised tax freedom for life (he and his descendants), and the King's daughter in marriage (a beautiful woman). Those are both benefits. He kept the benefits before him as a mechanism to eliminate his fear and act in courage. It has been said that fear is an acronym for False Evidence Appearing Real. When you continually repeat and rehearse rewards, the reward in your subconscious mind will cause the illusion of fear to go away. Compassionate samurai display courage simply because that is who they are, but you can increase the display of courage by creating very tangible rewards.

3. Support Group

All good is attacked. Remember that. Do not resist it. It is a part of the way the world is. Learn to display more courage than any attack can handle.

Support can help you do that. Do not go it alone. According to a zoologist in a fight between a lion and a tiger the tiger always wins. They have more fierceness and courage and heart. They will do anything to win. However when you have five tigers versus five lions the lions always win. Why? The lions work as a team and pick off the tigers one by one who refuse to work together.

You are a lion. Build a team. David's family, for even hanging out with the soldiers ridiculed him. He combated their negativity by "turning from them to another". Perhaps "another" meant God or perhaps "another" meant another human being. The book doesn't specifically say. For sure, whomever he turned to was supportive of him. When confronted by fear and negativity, a compassionate samurai looks for people who will affirm his or her greatness and the fact they can fearlessly move forward. After my mentor died, his wife took over, and the company changed.

I hung on for many years trying to change her and the company. I was afraid to leave because I had never done anything except be in the army and work for Tom. I did not see myself as an entrepreneur. I had three children, a wife and about $7,000 a month in bills. I was afraid to go out on my own. Things kept getting worse in the company from an integrity viewpoint as the years went on. Finally in a discussion with my wife, she asked, "What is the worst thing that could happen if you go out on your own?" I replied we could lose our house, our car, not be able to our bills. She replied, "It will be okay. If it happens I won't like it, but we will just buy another house and car. I want you to go on your own. You were meant to do this."

That support gave me the courage and I walked out with no business plan, took no one with me, started in a different arena with corporations instead of public seminars and we made money, and made a difference from day one. That was 11 years ago. Some of you do not have that family support. Work on creating it at home and actively create it elsewhere. Sometimes in network marketing and other businesses the spouse only sees that they see their spouse less often than before. No wonder they are not supportive. A compassionate samurai is a giver. Give your spouse what they want and they will give you support. Go to meetings and meet successful samurai like yourself. Make friends. Help them. Create your own pride of lions.

4. Leverage your strengths

In the story, David tries on the king's armor. It doesn't fit because he is small and only 16 years old. He goes back to what he is good at: sling shots. Even though that is very unconventional, he chose to focus on his strength. That increased his courage. In guerilla wars, the guerilla forces have the strength of mobility and speed. They capitalize on that. They avoid fixed confrontations because size and big equipment is not their area of strength, and they would get beat if they had to rely on that. Business is the same way.

What is your strength in business? Is it knowledge? Organizational skills? Creativity? Drive? How can you capitalize and leverage that strength? It does not mean you pretend you have no weaknesses. On the contrary, you know you and your weakness. Find a way to not make yourself vulnerable with them. What is your strength as a spouse or parent? How can you leverage that? That will give you confidence and courage.

5. If God is for you who can be against you?

Put aside your religious beliefs or doctrine for the moment. In the story, Goliath comes at David as one skillfully trained. Fighting was Goliath's profession. He had the better equipment, spear and shield. He was physically superior in size and strength. David's only defense is God. But that is enough. If God is infinite, regardless of your faith, what could stand up to that? You have a conscious mind, sub-conscious mind, and are connected to God through your spirit. In a three-part snowman God is the biggest of the three balls on the bottom, acting as the foundation.

Having infinite on your side is a definite confidence booster
that allows you to display more courage.

Is it possible to be financially successful in the world without God? Yes. Your sub-conscious is very powerful. But why would you cut off the largest part of you? It doesn't make sense. You are a spiritual being who has a body. A compassionate samurai explores his or her spiritual nature. They are comfortable with that part of themselves, and look to that part for guidance. Having infinite on your side is a definite confidence booster that allows you to display more courage. You would take anything on and a compassionate samurai does.

Everybody has viewpoints or ways of looking at things. For years we have referred to these viewpoints as sunglasses. People have many different ones, about nearly everything in life. You have a pair of sunglasses about what you believe about maintaining a healthy weight, having lots of money, relationships, children, getting a quality education, job stability, owning a business, taking vacations, and flying airplanes. People only make radical changes when they perceive that the benefits to the change are more rewarding than the prices if they remain the same.

Change will never come in a person's life unless they realize that change requires boldness. It really takes courage to make a change in your life especially when you have been a certain way for so long. I got married in my thirties. Up until that point I really wasn't involved in a whole lot of serious relationships with women. What I mean by serious relationships; is relationships that I felt had the potential to possibly lead up to marriage. That was the farthest thing from my mind. I had sunglasses around what I though about marriage and relationships.

For a compassionate samurai, **Courage is not optional.**

One of the reasons the traditional samurai appeared to be so fearless is that they played life as if they were dead already. This is not gloom and doom. It is very freeing. A person who has nothing to lose is not afraid of losing. They play with abandon, full out. If you started a business and you were not afraid of losing it you would go for broke. Hence the saying, "Go for broke". That way of thinking, frees you up to play totally full out in life. The same is true in a marriage or in any project

For a compassionate samurai, **Courage is not optional.** 'No courage' is an option but not having courage is a price the compassionate samurai is unwilling to pay. Body alive—spirit dead. When you don't operate in courage, a piece of you die. Every action lacking courage is like taking a knife and cutting yourself. The person ends up being a 45-year-old walking zombie. Just knowing that little piece of information would probably make you far more eager to continue on reading to discover why you really don't have a choice in the matter, if you desire to lead a meaningful life.

Succinctly put, you have to display courage. And if you lack in that area, do whatever it takes to get courage quickly! Average people generally tend to move forward in life when all of the conditions are optimal for them to go ahead. The problem with that mindset is that conditions are usually never conducive for going forward. What if Mother Teresa waited for the conditions in Calcutta, India to improve before she decided to minister to the needs of the poor and hurting souls in that region? She would have never started her ministry.

The greatest rewards are typically preceded by some of the greatest challenges. You don't just conquer valuable land filled with treasures without a fight, without blood shed. It's at the point of discovering the *cost factor* that most people tend to go into a clam's shell as they run for cover, trying to hide from the only thing that will free them from the bondage of mediocrity. You don't want to do it, because you are afraid. Average people are so focused on the cost they can't see the reward.

I have met many people who did not want to get married because they were afraid to commit to a lifetime of being faithful to the love of their lives. I know smart and talented men and women who are financially broke, yet have all of the know-how to run a successful corporation, yet they remain wanting simply because they are afraid. They say things like, "What if the business fails? What if I go bankrupt? Suppose nobody desires the services that I am offering? "What if she is not the one?" "How can I know this is the right thing to do?" What will I do?" those are all average/mediocre person questions. The compassionate Samurai asks, *"What will happen if I don't take the bold steps?"*

It really doesn't matter what the scenario is, whether it's your timidity about purchasing a piece of real estate, buying a new car, getting married, going into business, joining the church, taking on a board position, or even investing in the stock market. When you choose not to do what you set out to do, it's because you fail to see you have the courage to move forward past all of the stuff that you made up in your own mind. The cure—DO IT AFRAID! You have to learn to do what you have to do even if you are afraid. Fear in and of itself is really not your problem. Your problem is not facing your fears head on.

Just Before Your Greatest Breakthrough

Have you ever heard the story of Chuck Yeager breaking the sound barrier? It illustrates this point eloquently. Chuck Yeager is a member of the National Speakers Association and in his talks freely admits that he had fear. Chuck was a United States Air Force test pilot. He was the first person to fly faster than the speed of sound, breaking the sound barrier. This man operated with great courage. All of the pilots that tried to break the sound barrier knew that they could possibly die while they were accelerating if they weren't able to control the plane as it began to shake frenziedly through the air, unaccustomed to traveling at such enormous speeds.

He knew that he could have possibly been killed in the plane, but if he didn't push himself past that thought he never would have "broken" the barrier. For a compassionate samurai life is not about getting comfortable where you are right now. Average people have retirement and a comfortable life as their goal. For a compassionate samurai life is all about breaking barriers, going to the next level. Once you arrive at the place by displaying courage you'll have to pack up and move again. Courage has many addresses, which requires you to stay in motion. Courage is a continuous journey. It never stops.

Chuck Yeager knew two men had flown the same plane he was about to fly and had died trying to break the sound barrier. Courage is spitting in the face of your fear. As both men had flown their planes faster the plane shook more violently. Both men said, "I can't keep flying this fast and tried to slow down." In the process of slowing down they crashed and were killed. Chuck Yeager had the same experience. The faster he went the more the plane shook. The only thing that was different was how he thought. He said to himself, "If I am going to die, I am going to die in style." He tried to speed up instead of slow down. Boom!!!

He broke the sound barrier and his plane almost instantly went still. Almost always, right before you are going to breakthrough to a new level your plane or your body is going to shake violently. Think back to when you bought your first house. Your hand was probably shaking a little because of the large loan you were signing for. After you did it though, you tended to relax. Think back to when you were first dating. You were getting the courage to ask the person out and maybe your lips quivered a bit. After they said yes you were amazed it was so easy and wondered why you hadn't asked sooner. A compassionate samurai understands this principle and is not fooled into backing down as their life becomes turbulent and their fear level increases. It is a natural part of the order of things and separates the average person from the extraordinary results of a compassionate samurai.

When you are scared and want to back down is exactly the time you should go faster, forward, do more. When you are afraid you tend to slow down feeling as if you won't be able to do what you set out to do, so you retract. In the midst of your fear you must find a way, gain an inner incentive, to go faster than you ever have. A friend of mine, Aaron D. Lewis, likes to say, **"Fear runs much faster than courage, yet it never has enough energy to finish the race."**

The Many Faces of Courage

Courage is the determination not to be overwhelmed by any object, that power of the mind capable of sloughing off the thingification of the past.

—*Martin Luther King Jr., Where Do We Go From Here? 1968*

Courage comes in many different packages and has various faces. One such example of this is my dad. My father wasn't an entrepreneur or a best-selling author. Nonetheless, my dad is a great man who has displayed a great amount of courage. Towards the last years of my mother's life on earth, my father took care of my mother for nearly 2 years. My mother had gotten ill to the point where she had to be taken care of much like an infant. My dad changed her diapers, cleaned her, and stood by her until she died.

At some point it may have been right to take her to a convalescent home. Because of my mother's wishes he did not take her to a nursing home, but courageously did what he had to do to make it work. It was the courage to face a daily grind. Michael J. Fox is battling the endless slow loss of control of his body with Parkinson's disease and has been an inspiration to millions. Other people face a momentary event such as 9/11 where you display courage or you don't. No matter who you are, you can display courage in some way because it is in you.

Courage does not always have to be loud and obvious. Sometimes it is and sometimes it isn't. What is easy for one person to do can terrify another and vice versa. One person can do physical challenges with ease and yet be terrified to become vulnerable in a relationship. Another can easily be vulnerable and share their feelings, but be afraid to start their own business or take on a high-pressure job. Everyone has fears including those afraid to admit it. Your fear is your fear. Do not try and make sense out of it or compare yourself to anyone else.

How To Win at the Game of Life

Being unreasonable and illogical causes us to lose courage. Most Americans sincerely educate our kids to become survival oriented not recognizing that causes them to die. The average person is more worried about their kids emotionally, mentally, and don't want them to be hurt. They over protect them. Then the child begins to believe that playing not to loose is the game of life. "I just want to make sure that I don't loose my job. In a relationship I will be open with you if I can be guaranteed that you will not hurt me.

You can't win at the game of life trying to shelter yourself from every single hurt that may come your way. Some parents tell their adult children not to go into a potentially multi-millionaire business venture, but rather stay on their job for the sake of insurance benefits and a pension that they'll receive thirty years later. Winning at the game of life requires courage to do it, without knowing all of the facts. You have to make decisions from your gut and trust yourself and trust that God is leading you exactly where you belong.

You do have what it takes. The person that tries and keeps on trying will eventually get to where he or she is going. That person will become a compassionate samurai. The person that sits back and does nothing will always live at the lowest point in life, mediocrity. Mr. and Mrs. Average can be defined as the best of the worst and the worst of the best. It takes great courage to admit failure, yet try all over again. The lessons that you learn from your failures allow you to now take a different path.

A Word of Caution

Sometimes what looks like courage is actually an act to cover up cowardice or insecurity. A friend of mine, Azim Khamisa, had his son Tariq delivering pizzas, working his way through college. One night, a gang accosted Tariq and he refused to give up the pizza. The gang leader had a 14 year old shoot and kill Tariq. Shooting someone might seem like it took courage, but in reality the 14 year old was more afraid of the gang leader and being rejected by his peers then he was of being in prison. The courageous act would have been to refuse and stand up to the peer pressure.

Many acts are committed in the name of courage that is in fact not courageous at all. You must look at not only the act, but also what is driving the behavior. Azim, by the way, acted like a compassionate samurai and not only publicly forgave the 14 year old, but he reached out to the guardian and grandfather of the killer and in the common pain of both losing family members, formed a foundation together to stop kids from killing kids. That was a magnificent display of courage. (www.tkf.org)

Courage is the first of human qualities because it is the quality which guarantees the others.—Aristotle

Boldness

"Shall I tell you a secret of a true scholar?
Every man I meet is my master in some point and
in that I learn from him." —Emerson

Compassionate samurai are satisfied without being settled.

Average people are settled without being satisfied.

Chapter Ten

Knowledge

What do you picture when you think about a person who is knowledge-able? For the average person, when they think about someone that is knowledgeable they immediately think about book smarts, high grade point averages, Harvard and Yale Universities, or graduating at the top of the class. Others may think about people that work in specialized vocations such as scientists that work for NASA who can figure out how to make things fly to the moon and back or even brain surgeons that can dexterously separate Siamese Twins.

This tenth character trait of a compassionate samurai is so much more. This character trait does encompass specific knowledge, but it is also about a constant eagerness to learn and the practical wisdom of applying knowledge to your current situation to produce a desired outcome. A compassionate samurai realizes that specialized knowledge can provide an edge. They are constantly seeking knowledge and the experts to teach them on a wide diversity of topics to include technology, finance, relationships, personal growth, health, and leadership.

Don't Settle For What You Have

Average people are either arrogant and believe they are so smart they don't need to learn, or are complacent, thinking learning really isn't necessary. As I travel around the world I have run across literally thousands of people that as we start talking about our Personal Mastery or leadership seminars (go to www.Klemmer.com) say, "Why should I do a class? I am fine!" In reality their ego is out of whack and they are asking the wrong question. They are fine, but what are they settling for? Do you have to be broke to want more money? Do you have to have a marriage on the edge of divorce to want to make it better?

Let me ask you a question. Do dogs like bones? Most times when I ask that of an audience people respond, "Of course they do." I say, "No they don't". Dogs like steak, they just settle for bones. Think about it. If dogs were setting the table with the food, who do you think would get the bones? I think they would give us the bones and keep the steak for themselves, don't you? What happens is the dog gets fed bones, bones, bones, and more bones. Then they start thinking I like bones.

They start settling for bones instead of steak. It's not that they dislike bones or that bones are bad, it is that they are SETTLING for bones. Take someone who has been in a good marriage for 15 years—a good marriage, not a bad one. What they experience year after year is good marriage, good marriage, and more good marriage. It is relatively easy then to start settling for a good marriage instead of creating a spectacular one (the steak).

A compassionate samurai is about excellence always
seeking to surpass whatever level they are at.

I am NOT talking about changing who you are with, but making the relationship you 're in better. If you have a home, job, nice car, and make an amount of money that is on par or slightly better than most of your neighbors, it is relatively easy to start settling for a good income instead of creating a spectacular income. A compassionate samurai is about excellence always seeking to surpass whatever level they are at.

Being Satisfied Without Settling

Part of the challenge around this, is average people get confused and think that if I want more I must be dissatisfied with what I have. Not only is that belief untrue, but it also creates a box where to be motivated, I must be dissatisfied. Think about the insanity of that. It actually ties happiness to dissatisfaction. Talk about a rat stuck in a maze.

Average people think something will make them happy so they strive for that something only to achieve that something and find happiness is not there. The problem lies in that satisfaction does not reside in the same realm as more and better. This is a very deep issue that for most people must be experientially explored to fully understand.

THIS IS IT	MORE, BETTER, DIFFERENT
I'm Satisfied	I'm Gratified (excited)

Terms Defined

(This is it and I am satisfied) Satisfaction—is the feeling of being in alignment with your purpose.

(More better different) Gratification—is the feeling of achieving something. I achieve that feeling by getting more of something, something better, or something different than what I already have.

Think of something in your life you don't like. Perhaps you are in a boring marriage. Perhaps you don't find your job economically or financially rewarding. Maybe you are overweight. Or you may have an illness such as cancer. Pick something you don't like. Say to yourself "My marriage is boring and I am satisfied." "I am overweight and I am satisfied." Whatever the circumstance may be, and I am satisfied. If you are an ordinary person you almost get sick to your stomach saying this. "I can't say that. It's not true." You can and YOU MUST!

You resist saying that because somewhere deep within, you think your resistance will change things. It doesn't. *Your resistance not only doesn't change anything, it prevents you from creating what you want.* Non-resistance does not mean giving up or resigning yourself to something. The examples we used were of martial arts and non-resistance to a punch being thrown at you. You do not make the punch wrong. You do not resist it. It simply is. You adjust and flow with it. Thus you are able to turn the person and be in control.

When you resist you lose control. You lose your ability to create, which is over on the more-better-different realm. Think of satisfaction, as acknowledging something for how it is (the punch) with zero resistance. *Satisfaction or contentment is found in being where you are supposed to be.* It is being in alignment with your purpose. This requires two things 1) knowing your purpose and 2) understanding that there are an infinite number of mechanisms for any one intention.

Can you find a way to take the situation of being overweight work to support your purpose? Suppose your purpose was to make a difference or to be a friend, could you use the circumstance of having extra weight support you in being able to relate to more people? You could even make a difference and have more friends. So from that angle you are incredibly satisfied. You'll lose weight not to feel satisfied, you already are. Losing weight will produce a feeling of gratification, achievement. Are you getting the difference?

This allows the compassionate samurai to be satisfied or content whether the situation is one they like or don't like! What incredible liberty. The average person resists situations they don't like because with a scarcity mindset they can only achieve their purpose through a certain limited number of circumstances. Put this feeling, which we are calling satisfaction or contentment, over in the box or bucket on the left.

Now lets talk about the box or bucket on the right called more, better and different. Have you ever gotten a new car? How did you feel? It was a rush. Let's call that gratification. How long did it last? It probably lasted less than a few months. You may even experience frustration that it didn't last. Within a year they are trying to sell you a new car. You go out and want that rush or gratification and buy a new car. Serious problems are created when we confuse gratification with satisfaction and contentment.

When you are in alignment with your purpose things don't matter
unless they support your purpose.

That is what the average person does. The average person seeks satisfaction in losing weight, getting a new car, or more money. When they don't get satisfied from that they tend to lean toward depression. They confuse gratification, which is a feeling of achievement with being in alignment with purpose. When you are in alignment with your purpose things don't matter unless they support your purpose.

Gratification and satisfaction are in different realms or boxes. This is another one of those topics you can spend years understanding, so do not be concerned if you are not grasping this at first. As always, experiential learning is the best way to get this in your heart instead of your head. Some people when they first start looking at this say, "If satisfaction is not dependent on anything being different, why should I even bother with more-better-different?" That's a good question. The box of more and better is about creation. It creates momentum and a temporary excitement, that we call gratification.

In business, marriage, health, a compassionate samurai creates a game of more- better-different for the purpose of creating. The challenge is not to be in the scarcity of either one box or the other, but to operate from both boxes simultaneously. The left box involves being in the moment and yet the right box lies in the future creating new possibilities. Playing in both boxes is when you are most effective. Think of a great sports player. Usually they love the practice of the sport as much as the game. Masters love to practice until practice becomes a habit.

A superstar like Jerry Rice in football is usually the first on the practice field and the last off. He loves the practice. This is why as a compassionate samurai you make "practices" or daily habits of the ten traits. Think of a sports player when they talk about being in "the zone". They are totally in the moment (left box) they are masters adjusting to any circumstance producing what seems like miracle results in our eyes. At the same time they are in a game of more, better. The more better is not just about the other player or team, they are always striving for better **steak** (remember our dogs and bones).

The average person is trying to fill the satisfaction bucket with more-better- different. *You cannot fill the bucket of satisfaction with more better different.* This is why you can observe people with gobs of money, fame, and material success and they can still be very unhappy or unsatisfied. They are unfulfilled. Average people have not oriented their circumstances to their purpose but have gotten lost on the more-better-different side. If you push the satisfaction or contentment over into the right box you have built a context or system where you must always be unhappy to be motivated! Think about that as a box to live in. Remember this, to have proper balance in life you need both boxes always working simultaneously producing contentment and gratification.

Having A Beginners Mind

To excel at the more-better-different side is to excel at creation. To do that and be a compassionate samurai requires having a beginners mind. Having a beginner's mindset does not mean that you are in a perpetual state of learning the same thing over and over. Repeating the same lesson is not having a beginners mind. Repeating the same lesson over and over is more like having an insane mind.

"Insanity: doing the same thing over and again and expecting different results."
—Albert Einstein

There is nothing wrong with failure in life. In fact, coming from, "this is it and I am satisfied," a compassionate samurai does not resist their failure. They use the failure to draw closer to their purpose. They learn a lesson. Average people resist their failures and miss the lesson. Average people miss a golf shot and in resisting their "failure" tie their emotions and concentration to the past. Compassionate samurai release themselves from the failure, learn a lesson and immediately create a spectacular shot. When you fail to recognize why you have failed, you find yourself repeating your same failure all over.

The beginners mind says, "I've always got more to learn." It is a place of humility. No matter how much I know there is always more to learn. Say it now, aloud, *"I've always got more to learn"*. Saying that will either make you feel great or feel not so great. If you feel not so great after saying those words, it may be because you are dealing with a little bout of pride, which makes you think that you already know enough and there's really no need to learn anything more. This story will help to illustrate this point.

One day a young encyclopedia salesman knocked on the door of a potential customer. After waiting about two or three minutes an elderly man in his mid to late eighties opened the door inquiring why this young man was there. The young boy told him that he was selling encyclopedia sets with additional books on the best climates to live in America. If you purchased the set you'll get the additional books as a free gift. Wasting no time the old man quickly told the young lad, "No need taking out any of those books." At my age there is nothing more for me to learn. I've been around this mountain a few times and I've just 'bout seen it all. Besides that I've got a breathing condition that acts up in cold weather here in New England, causing me shortness of breath. Other than that I'm all right. I suppose I just got to live with the breathing problem since this here region ain't getting any warmer 'til summer time." With that he told the young man goodbye, wished him good luck and closed the door.

Little did this old man know that more than a dozen older men and women, suffering with the same condition that were offered this book offer, bought the books from the young encyclopedia salesman, read the free-offer book specifically dealing with the best climates in America, located the city of their preference for their condition, moved away and lived another enjoyable 25 years. The old man that refused the offer died the same month.

The other octogenarians saw this young salesperson as someone having something that they needed regardless of how young he was. They still wanted to learn more. They had beginners mind. If learning more meant that they needed to learn through someone perhaps one-quarter of their age that would be just fine. The old man that died, died for the same reason most people die, he stopped learning. You can die physically or you can die emotionally, spiritually, and mentally.

Here is the epitaph for the average man or woman. *John Average Man. Born 1900. Died 1940. Buried 1983.* Their body hangs around but they are dead. You have seen them in countless businesses and homes. They are 50-year-old walking zombies with no passion who have quit living and just merely exist. Some are even proud of it. They proudly state, "I am a survivor." Compassionate samurai are thrivers, not survivors.

Unlike the average person, the compassionate samurai is dedicated to a life of always learning more, knowing that there is always something more to learn. There is a statistic I have heard that the average person reads less than one self-improvement book a year after they graduate from school. Their mediocre mindset thinks, I had enough reading in school, now I'm not reading anymore unless I have to. Compassionate samurai have a voracious appetite to read educational books, listen to learning CD's and go to seminars.

When you have a beginners mind age is irrelevant, position in a company is irrelevant. Beginners mind is a high level of maturity. At this level you are not worried about your image. The compassionate samurai's only worry is "how can I get better?" I am open about where I need to improve. I am blind to my weak spots, if I don't have beginners mind. It is not so easy to have a beginner's mindset in the area of your so-called expertise. The average person wants to believe that they cannot learn anything more in the area that they specialize, in order to appease their ego.

A compassionate samurai cares more about learning than they do ego. A beginners mind does not mean you don't know anything. Despite that knowledge I am going to approach this with a brand new set of eyes. A manager for 10 years may lack a beginners mind. Not having a beginners mind will make you become obsolete. It's a dangerous thing to not stay a beginner. When you think you know it all, you cut yourself off from your source, because you force yourself to stay in the conscious mind—where knowledge resides. Whatever you conceive God to be is not even the beginning of God. You limit God.

Success is a good thing. But sometimes with success come not-so-good attitudes and ways. Success can make you cocky. When that happens you will inevitably begin to falter because you won't find the value in listening to others around you, especially those that you feel are beneath you. Having the knowledge of a compassionate samurai requires great humility. Remember: the compassionate samurai always seeks to learn more because he knows that there is always more to learn. And learning can come in various ways from people that may appear to be subordinate to us, not as smart as us, or even a total stranger.

Aikido demonstrates this principle probably better than any other sport. When you go into a dojo where they are practicing Aikido, there are no belts worn in the dojo. There is a specific reason for this. Titles from outside the dojo mean nothing. Years of experience in practicing the art mean nothing. It supports humility. They make everybody at the same level. In Japan they don't even have belts. That's an American thing. The Japanese people don't measure progress the way we do here in America. Not wearing belts and trying to determine rank, avoids comparison. Avoiding comparison forces you to look at a person for who they are.

You will be far more open to a person's instruction or advice, if you think that they may have something relevant to say or give to you. When you are totally enamored with yourself, it's very difficult to receive from others even if their instruction is life changing. You have to go humbly in this process. Sometimes pastors that lead a mega church of 10,000 members may tend not to listen to pastors with 150 members or less. What a grave mistake! Maybe the pastor that leads 150 or less may not have reached the capacity of leading 10,000 and maybe that is not his or her calling to do so at all.

Be humble enough to receive instruction from those that you may not have formerly wanted to receive from.

The pastor may have some very significant knowledge to share with his brother and peer in ministry. He or she may have experience or even experiences in ministry that outweighs having masses of people. Pride will cause one pastor to shut the other out, thinking that he is not on his level. This occurs in all professions. Be humble enough to receive instruction from those that you may not have formerly wanted to receive from.

Arch-enemy to knowledge—Low self-esteem

One of the main nemeses to beginners mind is low self-esteem. To elaborate on this could possibly take up an entire chapter, maybe even a whole book. Low self-esteem can be a problem by itself. But the connection to low self-esteem and a person that is against receiving knowledge is pretty interesting. People that have low self-esteem try their best to cover it up in a myriad of ways. Some people will buy extremely costly clothing to try to dress up their low feelings about themselves. Others try to purport an image that says, "I know that already" to conceal a deeper problem lurking within. When a person does not have a beginner's mindset it is often associated with a psychological problem with how they feel.

Right/Wrong Paradigm

Closely associated with the resistance to receiving knowledge with beginners mind is the right/wrong paradigm. A compassionate samurai lives outside of right and wrong as an experience. Note: that is very different than morality. The compassionate samurai has a high moral code as we have been discussing. Conduct is gauged against this code and is either right or wrong in terms of the code. What we are talking about here is right and wrong *as an experience.* This is very different. They experience their circumstances outside of it being the right or wrong experience.

If they are in circumstances of poverty they do not make that wrong, they simply apply the code to those circumstances. If they are in conflict or a "battle", they don't make being in battle wrong; they simply apply these character traits or code to the battle. If they are single they don't make being single wrong, they apply this code to being single. In this manner they are never in resistance to wherever they are and all their energy is available to them. In aikido if someone throws a punch at you, you do not respond, "They shouldn't do that, that's not fair." You simply say, "Oh this is how we respond to a punch".

If a kick is delivered it is simply a kick and this is the way to respond. Average people make many circumstances wrong and resist it. They accept it as being the way that it is, and then consume most of their energy in resistance leaving little to create with. Compassionate samurai do not look at their viewpoint as right and the other person's viewpoint wrong. That would be like standing on the wet green side of a mountain range talking to someone on the barren dry side of the same mountain range and arguing who is right. The compassionate samurai hears the other viewpoint, has no need to defend their own viewpoint, does not judge the other viewpoint, but simply takes it in as a viewpoint and looks for its usefulness or relevance to their situation.

That is why they are great at receiving feedback. Suppose a child says to their parent "Daddy you don't love me". A compassionate samurai doesn't argue why they do. A compassionate samurai thinks, "That's an interesting viewpoint. Why would they say that? What am I doing or projecting in such that they would say that? Do I need to change how I am expressing my love so that it is heard and not confused with something else?" The same occurs in business, marriage or any other arena. Average people argue their "right viewpoint" and nothing ever changes in their situation.

Watch Out For These Things

There are some dangers of not being open to knowledge and not having a beginners mind. Beware of these things and maintain the stance in life that you are committed to growth and development in every area of you life. Be committed to growing in knowledge, wisdom, and understating.

1. *We will be blind to the lesson that is available to us when we believe we know it already. Don't be a know it all. When someone thinks that they know everything they lose out on knowledge.*

2. *When we are not open to growth and having a beginners mindset we tend to alienate people. When we don't want knowledge people shy away from us and are reluctant to offer their viewpoint.*

3. *Life replicates itself. After a while the same people that we mentor begin to think that they know more than us. They close themselves off from what we have to offer.*

4. *When we think we know it we become casual and become off purpose. This reduces our effectiveness in the face of challenges.*

5. *We lose passion and the freshness of life.*

Specialized Knowledge

With a beginners mind and an eagerness to learn we acquire specialized knowledge. Have you ever heard the phrase, "If only I knew then what I know now?" The average person uses this phrase with regards to some mistake that looks foolish now because of increased knowledge. Back then without the knowledge it didn't look foolish. The increased knowledge gives us an edge.

When I first began my company I can remember selling a piece of real estate and giving away $60,000 needlessly in extra taxes for no other reason than I just didn't know that I could have saved money on the deal. There were people back then that had the knowledge that I needed but I did not even seek them out because I did not have this compassionate samurai mindset. Because of that I lost big. Quite obviously there was a profit on the property, a capital gain on which I would have to pay taxes.

My tax accountant suggested that I pay right away as I would simply pay it now or later. I thought all accountants were the same. Accountants all have the rules, but they do not have the same skill levels. Heeding his advice, I wrote the government the check out immediately. About a year later, I went on a search for an accountant, interviewing several that worked for my multi-millionaire friends. To my total surprise I discovered that there were several legal ways to avoid paying approximately $60,000 in taxes.

Learning the hard way, I found out that not all accountants are the same. They have different areas of expertise and different levels of creativity. Had I had a beginner's mindset in that situation, I would have been more eager to learn about taxes, not to become my own bookkeeper, but to at least know why I was doing what I was doing. I could have also asked questions of other people to compare and see if I was getting a deal or a literal steal (the IRS stealing money from me). I am a strong advocate for paying money to the professionals.

Average people out of their scarcity will not pay for great experts. They will do it themselves or hire the cheapest vendor. In their mind it is too expensive. Compassionate samurai are happy to pay top dollar for an expert. They just make sure they are getting expert advice and not simply being over-charged. Personally, if I did my taxes it would take longer, I would miss opportunities to save money, and I would lose the opportunity to make money while I was doing the taxes. I know what I am best at.

Having a beginners mind does not mean that you've got to do it your-self. It means that you need to seek out knowledge beyond yourself so that you can be prepared and armed with knowledge about what you are involved in. Even if someone does your financial books for you, you should still have a working knowledge of where your money is going and how it is being spent. Seeking out that basic knowledge is having a beginner's mindset because you are tapping into resources around you. The samurai connects knowledge to winning.

There are really two different areas of knowledge: Specific knowledge and paradigm shifts or revelations. Specific knowledge is always being on the cutting edge of topics such as finance, relationships, health, and spirituality. Lets look at the area of finance for a moment. What can you learn about earning money? What can you learn about saving money by playing the tax game better? What can you learn about protecting your money? Have you explored the best way to leverage your giving? Yes, you want to hire experts to help you.

There is no way, that if you are not in that profession, you can keep up with the latest information. But if you do not educate yourself, you will not know the questions to ask to get a qualified advisor, much less to design exactly what it is you want. When was the last time you read a book on relationships? Are you entering a phase of your life with new challenges such as parenting, or an empty nest at home, or taking care your parents? How much new information do you think has been discovered in the last ten years alone? What are they now saying about vitamins?

Do you even know what normal cholesterol levels are? What about blood pressure? The amazing thing is how little time it takes. A half hour reading a day for five days a week in five years would make you one of the most knowledgeable people in any area of knowledge. Yes, that requires discipline. Compassionate samurai are disciplined. Begin now. Set a time and a place for regular reading. Not everyone has the same schedules or rhythms.

My wife gets up every morning around 5:30 A.M. and reads for at least an hour. It fits her style, and I have heard many speakers say that is the way you should start your day. I have never been able to do that. I am more like a train. I am slow to get moving in the mornings, but once I am rolling I go for a long time. My preference is to read at night. If my wife tries to read at night she will only make it through a page or maybe two. I have executives in our company like Patrick Dean who currently heads up our facilitators that read during the day on a regular basis.

It fits his style and daily schedule. So the lesson is, find your time. Find your place. But do it consistently. Don't use your lifestyle as an excuse for not having a system. Now get a system for topics. Do you want to focus on one area for a year? Perhaps you want to take a different topic every month. Pick your books now. Be a good steward of your time by consciously planning your educational reading time. This doesn't mean this is the only time you will read. But there is an old adage, if you don't plan than you are planning for failure.

What about listening to CD's or cassettes? Some people just aren't into reading. Then listen to CD's and read. Maybe you can download your teaching material onto an MP3 player or DJ Ditty. Some people have made fun of me for years for all the tapes I always have in my car. When I drive to and from the airport, which I do regularly, or if I am driving around town on errands, I find this a great time to listen to material. Obviously, I can't take notes like I can when I am sitting at home, but it still leverages my time. Part of my physical workout at home is to peddle a bike for thirty minutes and to do stretching, sit-ups and pushups. That's another great time to listen to educational CD's.

All the above has been specialized knowledge for your head. Now let's talk about the second type of knowledge, having paradigm shifts or revelations in your belief systems. This kind can only be done through experiential learning. That means you are doing an activity where you have an experience that changes your viewpoint on something. Are you going to wait for life to hand you the experience you need to enhance your career, relationships, health, or spirituality?

Life is usually the most expensive teacher in terms of time, money and relationships. That is why I am very strong on people doing experiential workshops. It's the fastest, cheapest, most fun way to accelerate your growth. The quality friends you meet that have like-minded values alone is worth the time and money you spend. Some of the paradigms or beliefs I had that made me successful in the United States Military did not make me success-ful as an entrepreneur. That doesn't make the old beliefs wrong. I simply had the incorrect map or paradigm for the territory or life situation that I was in.

The paradigms I had that made me successful as an entrepreneur did not work to take a multi-million dollar company to a one hundred million dol-lar company. It is an ongoing life process of discovery. That is why I encour-age people to be in a seminar as a student *at least every six months. Every quarter is even more appropriate for most people.* That's beginners mind. That's what a com-passionate samurai does. Average people go to one seminar, think they are all the same and are done.

Think of yourself as your own company **You Inc.,** even if you work for someone else. If you work for someone else, that job is your main income stream, but you are still your own business. Any business owner worth any-thing will tell you they have a budget for developing their people. Organizational constraint theory basically says the size and effectiveness of any organization is gauged by two factors: its systems and its people. So take a percentage of your gross income just like a company and budget it for your personal growth. It's the smart thing to do.

I recommend you take at least 5% of your gross income and invest it in your development. If you make $50,000 dollars a year that would mean you spend $2,500 a year on books tapes and seminars. If you can, stretch to spend more, just like a fast growth company invests more. The higher the price seminar, generally, the more successfully financial the people are with whom you will be learning with. They make great friends.

Tapping Into Resources Around You

A compassionate samurai always realizes the potential in others. Other peo-ple's potential can be a benefit to them, and help them to overcome some very tough situations. They seek out knowledge and learn lessons from some of the most unexpected and overlooked sources. Some of the greatest knowledge that you can tap into exist right within your circle. You really don't have to travel far to receive knowledge especially if you are really open to receiving. But far too often the knowledge that is seemingly at your fingertips goes unnoticed. It is when you reject that kind of knowledge that you find yourself either repeating a lesson one too many times or missing out on a big opportunity in life all together.

Some of the greatest knowledge that you can tap
into exist right within your circle.

My wife, Roma sometimes gives me input on different matters, from spirituality to business concerns. But sometimes there is an unsubstantiated tendency to discount her particularly when it comes to business matters since she is not leading a business of her own. That's not what she wants to do. It's not where her heart is. Her heart is into the arts and painting, with which she is very talented. But since she doesn't do business on a daily basis I'll sometimes ignorantly not take her advice as seriously as I should.

The strangest thing is that her feedback is usually directly on target. And if I reject it I am rejecting assistance that I may desperately need. What you need may be around you, going unnoticed since it's not wrapped in the wrapping that you readily identify. Roma doesn't have to be a business expert in order to offer her valuable knowledge to me. In fact, there are times when a person that is not directly connected to the business or vocation that you do gives their advice on a particular subject.

It's a non-biased observation. Business people think business. Athletes think in terms of sports. Preachers think in term of evangelizing everyone everywhere. Educators think in terms of educating others and seeking funding to do so in the most efficient manner. There is great benefit to network with people that think like you do. There is an equally great benefit to get a viewpoint from someone that has a totally different perspective also.

Insight and Foresight

Even having the specialized knowledge is not enough. You may know of people that did very well in high school and in college yet can't seem to make ends meet, they can't even land a descent job. How is it that you can have great book knowledge but no ability to get things accomplished in the real world? Many people have knowledge, but can't connect to applying it in the particular circumstances they are living in. Other people learned knowledge that isn't applicable to their life. Other people don't have the courage to apply the knowledge they have.

Statistics show that most people that take real estate and stock seminars never do a deal. Compassionate samurai have the appropriate knowledge, the insight to see its application to their life and the courage to apply it. Insight is the ability to see past simply what your eyes see. The average person sees a house for sale and knows the asking price and the condition of the house. That's what can be seen with the eyes. A person with insight sees that, but creates significance out of how it relates to other information.

Insight leads to foresight. Foresight is the ability to see how things will develop before they develop. Knowledge and experience increase insight. After doing numerous stock or real estate deals a person can develop insight where they can just look at a property or stock and know they can make money. Their conscious and sub-conscious are in harmony so that they are accessing more than just the normal five senses.

The Oarsman and The Advisor

Once upon a time in the days of sailing ships, kings and queens, there were two men. They grew up on the same street and attended the same schools. They dated some of the same girls and went to the same social functions. One day they moved apart, but after many years ended up working on the same ship. One was a mere oarsman and the other was the king's advisor. The oarsman was jealous of the advisor's good job and believed he should be an advisor also. He had the same education, so why not? It just didn't seem fair.

The king overheard his complaining and when they got ashore said to the oarsman, "Go to the top of the hill and tell me what you see." The oarsman ran up the hill, looked around, came back down, and said that cats were fighting. The king asked, "How many cats?" After climbing the hill again the oarsman said there were 5 cats. "What colors were the cats?" asked the king. The oarsman climbed the hill again and upon returning said there were 2 black cats and 3 brown ones. "What type of cats are they?" After climbing the hill again the oarsman said they were "minx".

The king called the advisor over and said, "Go to the top of the hill and tell me what you see." Upon returning the advisor said, "There are 5 minx cats that are fighting. 2 are black and 3 are brown. A fellow owns them over the hill. The owner says if the cats are bothering you, he will put them inside. If you are inquiring because you admire them, he will give you one." Are you an oarsman or an advisor? An oarsman does what he is told.

He does a good job, but he only does his job. A compassionate samurai advisor looks at the big picture and in addition to doing his or her job, asks questions they think their boss might want or need to know. Regardless of your job or position you may be either an oarsman or an advisor. Organizations excel when they have many advisors. I look forward to crossing paths in our journey together as compassionate samurai and in sharing the battles and contributions you have made.

"Shall I tell you a secret of a true scholar? Every man I meet is my master in some point and in that I learn from him." —Emerson

About The Author

Brian Klemmer has studied leadership since being at the United States Military Academy (1968-1972). He is the author of four best-selling books—*If How To's Were Enough, We Would All Be Skinny, Rich and Happy, When Good Intentions Run Smack Into Reality:12 Lessons To Coach Yourself And Others To Peak Performance, and Eating The Elephant One Bite At A Time: 52 Weekly Lessons In Leadership,* Known for his humorous and practical style of communicating, Klemmer is one of todays most in demand speakers.

His character development and leadership seminar company, Klemmer & Associates Leadership Seminars Inc., has conducted its work for more than one hundred thousand people around the world influencing the lives of people in countries such as the United States of America, Saudi Arabia, Australia, Mexico, Spain, the Philippines, and Scandinavia. His clients includes well known corporations such as Aetna Life Insurance, American Suzuki Corporation, General Electric, Walt Disney Attractions, and distributors for more than a dozen network marketing and direct sales organizations.

Klemmer & Associates seminars are one of the few colloquiums that measures and produce measurable and long lasting changes in people. You can find out more about Klemmer & Associates by visiting us online at www.klemmer.com or by calling 1-800-577-5447.

BOOKS CITED OR RECOMMENDED

Clearly, Thomas. (1999). *Code Of The Samurai: A Modern Translation of the Bushido Shoshinshu of Taira Shigesuke.* Tuttle: North Clarendon

Frankl, Victor. (1977). *Man's Search For Meaning.* Pocket: New York

Gutteridge, Rene. (2007). *The Ultimate Gift:* movie edition with promotional DVD. Westbow Press: Nashville

Klemmer, Brian. (2005). *If How-To's Were Enough We Would All Be Skinny, Rich & Happy.* Insight: Tulsa

Klemmer, Brian. (2004). *When Good Intentions Run Smack Into Reality: Twelve Lessons To Coach Yourself and Others To Peak Performance.* Insight: Tulsa

Leonard, George. (1992). *Mastery: The Keys To Success and Long Term Fulfillment.* Plume: New York

Leonard, George. (1999). *The Way of Akido: Life Lessons From An American Sensei.* Plume: New York

Munroe, Myles. (2000). *The Burden of Freedom.* Creation House: Lake Mary

Stoval, Jim. (1991). *The Ultimate Gift.* River Oak: Colorado Springs

Thurman, Howard. (1963). *Disciplines of the Spirit.* Harper and Row: New York

Trump, Donald and Kiyosaki, Robert. (2006). *Why We Want You To Be Rich: Two Men One Message.* Rich Press: Scottsdale

Twist, Lynne (2003) *The Soul of Money: Transforming Your Relationships With Money and Life.* W.W. Norton: New York

Welch, Jack and Welch, Suzy. (2005). *Winning.* Harper Collins: New York